DEFINED

WHO GOD SAYS YOU ARE

A STUDY ON IDENTITY FOR KIDS

LEADER GUIDE
STEPHEN & ALEX KENDRICK
WITH KATHY STRAWN
LIFEWAY PRESS®
NASHVILLE, TN

ABOUT THE AUTHORS

Published by LifeWay Press®
©2019 Kendrick Bros., LLC
Used under License. All Rights
Reserved.

ISBN 9781535956796
Item 005814776

Dewey Decimal Classification
Number: 268.432
Subject Heading: Discipleship—
Curricula\God\Bible—Study
Dewey Decimal Classification
Number: 248.82
Subject Heading: CHRISTIAN
LIFE \ JESUS CHRIST—
TEACHINGS

Printed in the
United States of America
LifeWay Kids
LifeWay Resources
One LifeWay Plaza
Nashville, Tennessee 37234-0172

We believe the Bible has God
for its author; salvation for its
end; and truth, without any
mixture of error, for its matter
and that all Scripture is totally
true and trustworthy. To review
LifeWay's doctrinal guideline,
please visit
lifeway.com/doctrinalguideline.

All Scripture quotations are
taken from the Christian
Standard Bible ®
Copyright 2017 by Holman Bible
Publishers. Used by permission.

STEPHEN KENDRICK is an ordained minister and New York Times bestselling coauthor of *The Love Dare*, *The Resolution for Men*, and *The Battle Plan for Prayer*. He has spoken in numerous countries to students, families, and men's groups. He is also an accomplished actor, screenwriter, and film director, whose credits include *Facing the Giants*, *Fireproof*, *Courageous*, *War Room* and *Overcomer*. He and his wife, Christina, have six children.

ALEX KENDRICK is an ordained minister who has served families for 20 years in student ministry and associate pastor positions. Along with his brother Alex, he is also a screenwriter (*Facing the Giants*, *Fireproof*, *Courageous*, *War Room*, and *Overcomer*), movie producer, and coauthor of three New York Times bestselling books (*The Love Dare*, *The Resolution for Men*, and *The Battle Plan for Prayer*).Stephen and his wife, Jill, have six children.

KATHY STRAWN has been writing kids' curriculum for LifeWay Kids for over 40 years, including kids' versions of the Beth Moore Bible studies: *Jesus the One and Only* and *The Beloved Disciple* and Priscilla Shirer's *Unseen: The Armor of God for Kids*. She has taught Sunday School and discipleship classes for children for many years at First Baptist Church, College Station, Texas, and now assists her husband in their Ministry of Education by consulting with churches about their children's programs.

TABLE OF CONTENTS

ADMINISTRATION GUIDE

LEADER GUIDE—*Defined: Who God Says You Are* (005814776) is an eight-week Bible study guiding kids to discover their identity in Christ, based on selected passages from Ephesians. The study can be used in church for any size group or in a family setting. This book provides detailed plans for each of the eight sessions. During the eight sessions, kids will learn that God defines who they are. They can learn how God defined their identity as image bearers of Him, how their identity was broken by sin, and how Jesus transforms their identity when they trust in Him. They will also learn about the new identity given to every believer and how Christ redefines their identity in Him.

ACTIVITY BOOKS—Because of the nature of the study, each child will need her own activity book. *Defined: Who God Says You Are Younger Kids Activity Book* (005814773) and *Defined: Who God Says You Are Older Kids Activity Book* (005814775) include 80 pages of activities designed to guide kids to learn about their identity in Christ. Games, activities, puzzles, deeper study guides, journaling pages, and parent pages are provided for kids to support each of the eight sessions of *Defined: Who God Says You Are*.

PRINTABLES—Included in this Leader Guide is a download code to access 32 printables to aid in teaching. To access your free downloadable items, go to my.lifeway.com/redeem and register or log in.

Enter this unique code to download your printable items: **5PJSJNZX2I**

1. Administration Guide
2. Family Guide
3. Allergy Alert
4. Key Passage Poster
5. Temptation Scenarios
6. Q & A Cards
7. Clap and Stomp
8. Gospel Statements
9. Mix and Match
10. Ephesians 2:8-9 Cards
11. Human Vine Assignments
12. Speed Stack Memory Verse Strips
13. Balloon Display
14. The Vine
15. Lost Things Pictures
16. Spiritual Blessings
17. Prayer Sheet
18. How's Your Memory?
19. Peter Did
20. Prayer Posters
21. Greek Letters
22. Stinky Feet! Game Pieces
23. Stinky Feet! Review Questions
24. Three Corner Game
25. You've Got Mail
26. Letter to the Galatians
27. Letter to the Ephesians
28. Ephesians 2:2 Verse Cards
29. Ephesians 2:3 Verse Cards
30. Walking, Walking
31. A Soldier and His Armor
32. Dress the Soldier Questions

HOW DO I GET STARTED?

- Pray. Ask God to guide your planning, preparation, teaching, and follow-up for the study. Thank God for the opportunity to teach boys and girls how to grow closer to Him throughout their lives. Pray that God will grant you great love for the children who will come to the study.

- Choose a meeting time and place. Consult your church staff, if needed. Consider meeting during a time when adults and students are already studying *Defined: Who God Says You Are*. See page 104 for more information about these products. If you choose this plan, find out how long the adults and students will meet each week. If they meet for more than an hour, think about adding time for snacks as well as planning to use all of the suggested activities each week. However, kids can attend and learn from this study at any time. Try to find a meeting area that is large enough for the number of kids you expect so they can play active games and have fun.

- Gather resources. Order the resources mentioned on the previous page.

- Recruit workers. Find at least one person to help you. Many churches require at least two adults to be in a room with kids. This is for both the kids' protection and yours. One worker for every 10 kids is a good goal. If you expect more than 15-18 kids, enlist enough workers to form two classes, possibly one for younger kids and one for older kids. Ask God to direct you to people who are experienced children's workers and faithful Christians. Explain to potential teachers what you expect from them, what their responsibilities would be for both planning and teaching, and the dates and times of the classes.

- Determine your schedule. If possible, try to arrange 8 weeks in a row to maintain consistency in learning. If that is not possible, try to line up sessions as close together as you can.

- Plan ahead. Meet with other leaders to decide who will do each part of the session. (See *What Happens at Each Meeting?* in the next section.) Print out teaching aids from the downloadable items. Cut apart items from the copies. Clip the pieces of each item together or place them in resealable bags. Gather supplies. A list of items needed for each activity is printed in each session.

WHAT HAPPENS IN EACH SESSION?

Each session is divided into the following parts:

INITIATE (INTRODUCTION) — As soon as they arrive, kids will play games or do quick activities to peak their interest in what they will learn during the session.

INQUIRE (BIBLE STUDY) — Kids will hear a Bible story, learn about a specific part of their identity to grow closer to God, discover how to put into practice the specific ways they learn, review the memory passage, pray, and apply Biblical truths to their lives.

INVESTIGATE (BIBLE STUDY ACTIVITIES) — Kids will participate in activities that help them internalize the learning and express ways they can use what they learn. Two activities are suggested for each session. You may use these in different ways: Form small groups to work with different teachers at the same time or conduct both activities consecutively. This is also a perfect time to go through the Activity Books to dive deeper into the discussion.

INCREASE (CONCLUSION) — During this time, kids will review both the Bible story and the application of what they studied during the session. They will have a prayer time and end the session with an active game related to what they have studied.

SHARING THE GOSPEL RESOURCES

The ABCs of Becoming A Christian (CSB: 005125105) is sold in packs of 25 and provides helpful information about how to become a Christian. Also available in KJV (005125106).

The Gospel: God's Plan for Me (CSB: 005567177) is sold in packs of 10 and emphasizes God's plan of salvation from Creation to Jesus and how we respond to the good news. Also available in ESV (005567178).

SHARING THE GOSPEL WITH KIDS

Some kids who participate in *Defined: Who God Says You Are* may not have made a personal decision to accept Jesus as Savior yet. This study could present you with just the right setting for sharing God's plan with kids. Consider these thoughts as you get ready to share.

- The ultimate goal of teaching the Bible is for a person to accept Jesus as his Savior when the Holy Spirit leads him to realize that he has sinned against God and is spiritually lost. The Holy Spirit is the leader in the experience, but believers have the responsibility of following the Spirit's leading.

- Becoming a Christian is an individual matter and discussions about conversion are more effective when conducted individually. The child will feel freer to share true thoughts and feelings.

- If a kid indicates a desire to become a Christian, ask her to tell you what she feels. Use questions that require thoughtful answers rather than just yes or no. Use language the child understands.

- Use your Bible as you share the gospel. After reading a Bible verse, be ready to explain the verse in your own words. Help the child understand unfamiliar terms such as repent. Refer to "The Gospel: God's Plan for Me" to help you know Bible verses to share and kid-friendly ways to explain how to become a Christian.

- Help the child know how he can respond. Use directions such as: Tell God you know you have sinned and are sorry. Ask God to forgive you for your sin, for wanting your way instead of God's way. Ask Jesus to become your Savior (the One who keeps you from being separated from God) and Lord (the One in charge). Again, refer to *The Gospel: God's Plan for Me* for good ways to help kids know what they can do.

- One common misconception for kids is that being baptized makes them a Christian. Be sure they know the difference between becoming a Christian, being baptized, and joining the church.

- Include parents or caregivers when possible. Tell them what led you to discuss salvation with their child. Explain where you think the child is in his spiritual journey (e.g. becoming aware of a need for God, is thoughtfully considering how to respond, made a decision to accept Christ, or wants to be baptized).

- Pray. Ask God's leadership as you help boys and girls grow in their understanding of salvation.

Created by God

KEY VERSE: "FOR WE ARE HIS WORKMANSHIP, CREATED IN CHRIST JESUS FOR GOOD WORKS, WHICH GOD PREPARED AHEAD OF TIME FOR US TO DO."
EPHESIANS 2:10

THROUGH THIS STUDY, KIDS CAN ...

KNOW

God created people in His image and for His glory.

UNDERSTAND

God has the authority to determine our identity and purpose.

DISCOVER

The Bible helps us know what being created in God's image means.

INITIATE

You Will Need:
Item 1: "Administration Guide"
2 sheets of yellow paper, 2 sheets of blue paper, tape

To Do:
Before the session begins, read the administration guide to help you lead each session.

Attach each sheet of paper to a different wall or as far apart as practical on one wall.

Teaching Tip:
If your space is small, make a tape line on the floor. Direct kids to straddle the line and move from left to right to show their choices rather than moving to different signs.

If your group is mostly older kids, consider directing them to move to the correct signs within 3 seconds.

WHO I AM

- Call attention to the papers on the walls. Tell kids you will make statements and assign a color to go with the answers. Explain that kids will move to the color sign that describes them. Kids should return to the center of the play area before the next statement is given.

- Name one of these choices and direct kids to the colors that show their answers.

  - If you have blonde or brown hair, move to the yellow sign. If you have black or red hair, move to the blue sign.
  - If you like pizza best, move to the blue sign. If you like chicken nuggets best, move to the yellow sign.

- Continue using these choices: smelling cinnamon or smelling vanilla, swimming or playing video games, skipping or running, blue/green eyes or brown/black eyes, playing board games or working puzzles.

- Comment that during this Bible study, kids will learn that God made each of them in His image and for His glory. Explain that kids can learn more about what being made in God's image means as they study the Bible.

INQUIRE

You Will Need:
Item 4: "Key Passage Poster"
6 note cards, markers or pens, scissors,

To Do:
On each note card, print a different Bible reference from this list:
Genesis 1:3-5; Genesis 1:6-8; Genesis 1:9-12; Genesis 1:13-19;
Genesis 1:20-23; Genesis 1:24-25.

Print the "Key Passage Poster" and display each verse on a large focal
wall. Print 1 additional copy of verse 10. Cut verse 10 apart to make 6
different phrases: *For we are His workmanship; created in Christ Jesus; for
good works; which God prepared; ahead of time; for us to do. Eph. 2:10*

Teaching Tip:
If you teach a small group of kids, let them work in pairs, but give them
two cards to research.

OPEN UP: TRACK THE DAYS

- Form ~~six~~ *Two* groups. Give each group a paper and markers. Explain that kids
  have probably heard the story of creation many times, but today they will
  research the Bible verses printed on their cards. Lead kids to work in their
  groups to find and read the Bible passage together. Kids will record on the
  papers what God made in their assigned verses. Allow several minutes of
  work.

- Call the groups back together. Let each group share their findings and
  post their paper on the wall. Note for kids that no one shared when
  people were created.

- Explain that God created everything for His glory, and He made people
  special from the rest of creation. He made us in His image. Ask kids what
  they think it means to be made in God's image.

- Open your Bible to Genesis 2:1-25. Tell the following Bible story in your
  own words or use the story provided.

do pg 7

TELL THE BIBLE STORY: CREATED BY GOD

On the sixth day of creation, God created people. He said, "Let's make man in our image. They will rule over the whole earth and take care of all living creatures."

2. So God made man and woman in His image. God formed the man, Adam, from the dust of the ground. God breathed into him the breath of life. Adam became a living being. God placed Adam in the Garden of Eden where all kinds of trees grew. A river watered the garden. Adam worked the garden and took care of it. God told Adam, "You may eat from any tree in the garden except the tree of the knowledge of good and evil. If you eat from it, you will die."

Then God said, "It is not good for the man to be alone." So God decided to make a helper for the man. God brought all the animals to Adam, and Adam named them. But none of the animals was a good helper for the man. So God put Adam into a deep sleep. He took one of the man's ribs and closed the man's side. God took the rib and made a woman!

God took the woman to Adam. Adam was extremely happy when he saw Eve. "This one, at last," he said, "is bone of my bone and flesh of my flesh."

The woman was a perfect helper for the man; she was his wife.

God blessed Adam and Eve and provided everything they needed.

That was the end of the sixth day. On the seventh day, God stopped creating and rested because He had completed His work.

— based on Genesis 1–2

MAKE THE CONNECTION

- As our Creator, God determines the value and purpose of His creation. In other words, God has the authority to define what is true about His creation. He defines its identity.

- Remark that a person's true identity is who God says he or she is. Read Colossians 1:15-17 aloud. Tell boys and girls that since Jesus has all power and authority, He has the authority to determine who we are and our purpose in life. He has the authority to determine our identity.

DEEPER STUDY

- Point out that being made in God's image means to have some characteristics that are like God, or to be patterned after Him. Ask kids to raise their hands if they have the ability to think and reason. Mention that thinking and reasoning is one way people are made in God's image. Ask kids to raise their hands if they can make choices. Note that making choices is a way people are made in God's image. Ask kids to raise their hands if they have the ability to make promises. Continue with these questions: Who can be creative? Who can learn right from wrong? After each one, remark that it is a way people are made in God's image.

- Remind kids that God does not have a physical body; He is Spirit, and He has given each of us a spirit. (See John 4:24.) God gives people the ability to think and to feel emotions and to make choices. He gives us the ability to understand right and wrong. In this way we are made in His image.

- Explain that we can learn about being made in God's image throughout the Bible, not just in Genesis. Direct kids to locate Ephesians 1:1 in their Bibles. Tell kids the Book of Ephesians is a letter to people who lived in the city of Ephesus. The letter was written long after God created the world. It was written several years after Jesus returned to heaven. Read the verse together. Help kids decide from the verse who wrote the letter and who received the letter. Tell kids that Paul wrote this letter while in prison for telling people about Jesus. Point out that the saints, in this verse, are people who have trusted Jesus as Savior. Paul was writing to the Christians in Ephesus.

- Remark that Paul's letter teaches more about God's creation of people. Direct kids to Ephesians 1:4. Ask, "When did God plan for people?" *(Before He created the world)* Continue directing kids to the different verses and asking the appropriate questions:

  - (v.7) What can Jesus provide for a person? *(redemption and forgiveness from sin according to His grace)*
  - (v.20) Who raised Jesus from the dead? *(God the Father)*
  - (vv. 20-22) What did God put Jesus above? *(everything)*

- Point out that kids expressed characteristics about themselves as they played the opening game, telling what they were like. Remind kids that all people are made in God's image and for His glory. Being made in God's image is not really about how we look; it is about who we are and what God created us to do.

- When we say God created us in His image, it means we have many similar qualities to God. He gave us these qualities so that we could glorify Him in unique ways. We can use our intelligence, emotions, and creativity to

think about, love, and worship God. Our identity is who God says we are. Explain that we will learn more about our identity throughout this study.

• Lead kids to find Psalm 139:13-14 in their Bibles. Let volunteers tell from verse 14 the results of how God formed them *(wonderfully made)*. Explain that God made people in just the right way to accomplish God's plan for them.

• Direct kids to Acts 17:24-25. Ask what these verses teach us about God. *(God made the world and everything in it; He has all authority; He is the Creator of everything.)* Direct kids to read verse 26. Ask what this verse teaches us about people. *(From Adam, God has made every nation; God has determined the time and boundaries of where people live.)* Explain that God chose everything about us—who we are, where we are, when we live—for His purposes and His glory.

Activity BFC

MEMORIZE

• Explain that during the study, the group will work to memorize Ephesians 2:1-10. During this session, kids will work to memorize the last verse of the passage because it sums up the whole passage.

• Display the verse strips created for the opening activity in order. Lead the group to read the verse aloud together. Explain that all people are made by God and for His glory. People are created in God's image. Point out that Ephesians 2:10 teaches God planned for people to do good works. God prepared the way ahead of people. He wants people to live according to His plan.

• Lead the group to read the verse aloud together several times. Form two groups and let them alternate turns to read the verse phrases. Then remove one section. Direct kids to read the verse again, filling in the missing section. Replace the section and remove a different section. Continue several times. Then stop replacing sections as kids repeat the verse. Keep going until kids are saying the verse from memory.

PRAY

• Ask what people often do when they are in the presence of kings or other important people. *(Answers may include kneel, bow, or shake hands.)* Suggest kids kneel as they pray to remind them that God is the One who created them. Guide kids to pray silently as you suggest prayer prompts.

• Say, "Praise God for two characteristics that describe Him." Pause as kids pray quietly. Continue in the same way with these suggestions: "Thank God for a way you are made in His image. Think about the way God made you to be and thank Him for making you exactly who you are." End with "Amen."

INVESTIGATE

You Will Need:
Activity Books, pencils

- Transition kids into small groups, leading them to form an older group and a younger group. If you have a large group of either older or younger kids, form groups of about 5 or 6 kids. Distribute the Activity Books and pencils. Direct the boys and girls to write their names on the inside front cover.

- Explain to the group that each week they will have pages in the Activity Books to complete. Call attention to the puzzles and fun activities that can help them learn more about God and their relationship with Him. Also point out the daily pages where they can write about what they are learning.

- Complete the Activity Book activities for this session. As kids work, talk with them about today's Bible story and about being created in the image of God. Point out the pages for kids to complete at home. Explain that working on these pages can help them learn more about being created in God's image. Encourage kids to continue their study during the coming week.

MAKE AND PLAY A GIANT SHUFFLEBOARD GAME

You Will Need:
Item 4: "Key Passage Poster"
Masking tape, a yardstick, a CD, and the Ephesians 2:10 phrases used during group study

Teaching Tip:
If you have carpet rather than a smooth floor, make the game on a large sheet of paper, or make a smaller version of the game on a tabletop and use a ruler and a coin.

- Suggest the group make a shuffleboard game to help them continue learning Ephesians 2:10.

- Guide kids to create the gameboard on the floor using tape: Mark a triangle base about 5 or 6 feet long. Starting at the middle of the baseline, use tape to make a vertical line about 6 or 7 feet tall. Connect each end of the baseline to the top of the vertical tape. Make two tape lines across the triangle so that you form six different sections on the gameboard. Let kids add another tape line to designate the beginning of the sliding zone about 1 foot below the baseline.

- Direct boys and girls to locate Ephesians 2:10 in their Bibles. Read the verse aloud together. Review the meaning of the verse. *(All people are made by God. People are created in God's image. God planned for people to do good works. God prepared the way ahead of people. He wants people to do His plan.)*

- Place the memory verse phrases in order to the side of the gameboard.

- Form two teams. Explain that kids will take turns kneeling at the sliding zone line and using a yardstick to push a CD forward. Assign each section of the gameboard a number from 1 to 6 with lower numbers at the bottom of the triangle. When the CD lands in a section of the gameboard, kids on the team repeat that many phrases of the memory verse. Teams can earn the same number of points as the number of sections they repeat. No points are awarded if the CD goes outside the zone. The first team to reach 20 points wins.

- Play the game. During the first couple of rounds, kids may look at the printed phrases and read them. After that, announce that kids may double their earned points if they can say the phrases by memory. Play the game for as many rounds as time allows.

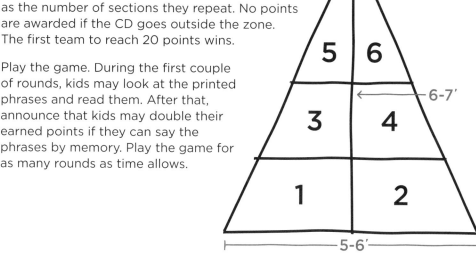

tape line marks beginning of sliding zone
(all black lines made with tape)

CREATE DUCT TAPE ID TAGS

You Will Need:
Plain paper, clear packing tape, duct tape in different colors and/or designs, scissors, hole punch, pens or pencils, cardstock cut into 1-by-2-inch rectangles, and leather cord or plastic lacing

To Do:
Practice making an ID tag holder before the session. Provide a flat, smooth work space.

Teaching Tip:
Younger children may need help folding their tape without leaving wrinkles. Assure them that the wrinkles will not hurt their project. Assist them in trimming edges.

- Direct kids to locate Ephesians 1:4 in their Bibles. Call on a volunteer to read the verse. Remind kids that God had a plan for them and all people before He created the world.

- Ask kids to recall different ways they are made in God's image. *(Ability to think; have a spirit, can make choices, creative, knowing right from wrong)* Print each answer on a sheet of paper.

- Suggest the kids make ID tags to remind them that their identity—who they are—is who God says they are.

- Give each kid three 6-inch pieces of packing tape to fold in half sticky-side to sticky-side, keeping the tape as smooth as possible. Assist kids in trimming their tape to about 1½ inches by 2½ inches. Explain that the tape pieces will become windows for the ID tag holder. Kids will position one window on the front of their ID tag holder, and two more inside.

- Distribute one 14-inch piece of duct tape to each child. Help kids fold the tape in half, sticky side to sticky side, to form a 7-inch piece and then in half again to about 3½ inches. Kids need to press down the folds. Guide the kids to position one of their clear tape windows on one side of the folded tape. Let the child place a little tape on each side of the window to hold it in place. Then the child may use a thin tape strip along each long side to seal the edge, then do the same to the other edge. (This will also help to anchor the window in place.) Repeat with windows inside the ID tag holder.

- Instruct the kids to use several of the cards and to print their name and information about what they are like, such as hair and eye color, something they like to do, or something they like to eat. Encourage kids to write, "I am who God says I am" on the front of their card. That card slides into the clear pocket on the front of the tape pouch.

- Lead the kids to write other cards to go inside of the pouch. Explain that these cards will have information about ways they are created in God's image. *(Ability to think; have a spirit, can make choices, creative, can learn right from wrong)*

- Kids will place these cards inside the pouch. Let kids punch holes in a top of the ID pouch, then add a leather cord to tie the pouch to a suitcase, backpack, or lunch bag.

- Challenge kids to remember both the ways they are made in God's image and the ways they have identity in Jesus.

DUCT TAPE FOR ID TAG

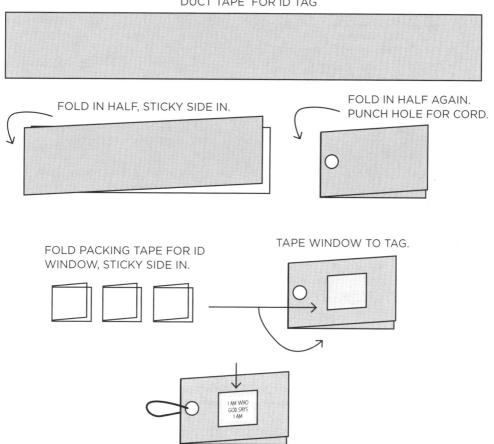

FOLD IN HALF, STICKY SIDE IN.

FOLD IN HALF AGAIN.
PUNCH HOLE FOR CORD.

FOLD PACKING TAPE FOR ID
WINDOW, STICKY SIDE IN.

TAPE WINDOW TO TAG.

I AM WHO
GOD SAYS
I AM

INSERT CARDS INTO TAPE POUCH.

INCREASE

You Will Need:
Item 2: "Family Guide"
Bell (or other noise maker), aluminum foil, a permanent marker, and a gift bag or bowl

To Do:
Cut 14 foil strips about 1-inch wide. On 5 strips, draw a star. On 5 strips, draw a question mark. On the other strips, print these Bible references: Ephesians 1:4; Ephesians 1:22; Genesis 1:27; Genesis 2:7. Place the foil strips in the bag.

Teaching Tip:
Use these review questions with the foil strip activity.
- When did God decide to create people? (*Before He made the world, Ephesians 1:4*)
- What is a way people are made in God's image? (*Ability to think, have a spirit, can make choices, can know right from wrong, creative*)
- From what did God create the first man? (*Dust, Genesis 2:7*)
- From what did God create the first woman? (*Man's rib, Genesis 2:21-22*)
- Who wrote the Book of Ephesians? (*Paul, Ephesians 1:1*)

- Instruct kids to begin walking around the room in random ways as they listen to these instructions: When you hear the bell, find another person and ask, "Who are you?" That person must answer the question without using the word "I" or her name. Then she asks you, "Who are you?" You must respond without using "I" or your name. Tell kids that if their partner does use her name or "I," she may make a loud wrong-answer beep.

- Suggest kids use answers such as "a lefty," "a soccer player," or "someone who likes to read." When kids hear the bell again, they will begin walking until the bell sounds again. This time, each child must find a different person to partner with for the questions and answers. Keep playing until kids have had four or five turns to answer.

- Explain God made each of us uniquely, but He made all of us in His image. We can know that God, in His authority, determines our identity and our purpose. Call on a volunteer to thank God for making people in His own image and for providing the Bible to help us know more about what that means.

- Present the bag of foil strips. Call for a volunteer to gently remove a strip from the bag. Explain that if the strip has a star on it, the group will repeat Ephesians 2:10 together. If the foil strip has a Bible reference on it, everyone will locate the Bible verse and one person will read it aloud. If the strip has a question mark on it, the child who chose the strip will choose a review question to ask the group. Keep playing until all the strips have been chosen.

- As kids leave, remind them to take their Activity Books and complete this week's activity pages at home. Assure kids they will not have to share any personal information or thoughts they record in their books. Challenge them to remember to bring their books with them for the next session.

- Point out the session's Family Guide located in the back of the Activity Books. Remind kids to complete this session's "Family Guide" with an adult at home. If kids don't take their books home, print a "Family Guide" for this week's session from the printable items and distribute as parents arrive.

Broken by Sin

KEY VERSE:
"AND YOU WERE DEAD IN YOUR TRESPASSES AND SINS."
EPHESIANS 2:1

THROUGH THIS STUDY, KIDS CAN ...

KNOW	**UNDERSTAND**	**DISCOVER**
Sin is to think, say, or behave in any way that goes against God and His commands.	All people are broken by sin.	Before trusting Jesus, our identity is broken by our sin and rebellion against God.

INITIATE

You Will Need:
Markers, a small bag, music, and music player
A sheet of paper and a small square of paper for each child

To Do:
Number the sheets of paper and squares of paper. Place the squares in the bag.

Teaching Tip:
Instead of playing music, create a clapping rhythm. Kids walk as long as the rhythm continues and then stand on a number when the clapping stops.

If you teach older kids, consider playing the game in teams. Put half of the numbered squares in one bag and the other half in another bag. When the music stops, choose a number from each bag. The kid who can name a rule first earns 100 points for his team. Challenge teams to be the first to earn 1000 points!

RULES EVERYWHERE!

- Welcome kids as they arrive. Instruct the kids to place the numbered sheets of paper on the floor all over the room. Explain that when you begin to play music, kids should walk around the room. When the music stops, each kid should stand on a numbered paper, but no one should be sharing a paper. Begin playing music. Stop the music and let kids move to the numbers.

- Tell the group that you will pick two numbers from the bag, and the kids standing on those two numbers will be the first to answer your question. Choose two numbers from the bag and indicate which kids will try to answer.

- Ask them to tell a rule they are asked to follow from their school or at home. After the kids respond, begin the music again. Continue playing until several kids have shared rules. Other options for questions are to tell rules at sports practice, the swimming pool, or riding a bike.

- Emphasize that kids have rules to follow in most places they go. Point out that adults also have rules to follow. Challenge the kids to listen closely to today's story to identify a time when someone did not follow God's rules.

Trespasses

INQUIRE

You Will Need:
Item 4:"Key Passage Poster"
Item 5: "Temptation Scenarios"
Dry erase board and marker

To Do:
Print Ephesians 2:1 on the dry erase board.

Teaching Tip:
If you do not have a dry erase board, print Ephesians 2:1 on a sheet of paper. Let kids cross out a word rather than erase it during the activity.

OPEN UP: TOSS IT

- Place two tape marks on the floor about 10 feet apart. Choose a volunteer to select one of the objects and toss a penny.

- If the penny lands on heads, the volunteer must walk from one tape line to the other while balancing the object on her head. If the penny lands on tails, she must balance the object on one foot while walking to the line.

- Allow each child to have a turn. For large groups, instruct several children to move simultaneously. Lead kids to identify which objects were the most difficult to balance.

- Comment that following God's instructions is not always easy, but it is always right. Today, we will discover more about our identity—who God created us to be. God created us in His image and for His glory, but we disobeyed God. Because of our disobedience, our identity is broken.

- Guide kids to open their Bibles to Genesis 3. Tell the following Bible story in your own words or use the story provided.

TELL THE BIBLE STORY: ADAM AND EVE SINNED

One day a serpent approached Eve and asked, "Did God really say, 'You can't eat from any tree in the garden?'"

Eve corrected the serpent: "We may eat fruit from any tree except one in the middle of the garden. God said, 'You must not touch or eat that fruit, or you will die.'"

The serpent told Eve, "You won't die! In fact, God knows that when you eat it, you will be like Him, knowing good and evil."

Eve looked at the fruit on the tree. She remembered that the serpent said the fruit would make her wise. Eve took some of the fruit and ate it. She gave some to Adam, and he ate it, too.

Immediately, Adam and Eve realized what they had done. They tried to cover themselves and hide from God.

That evening, God called out to Adam, "Where are you? Did you eat from the tree I commanded you not to?"

Eve said, "The serpent tricked me, and I ate it."

God told the serpent, "Because you have done this, you are cursed more than any other animal. You will move on your belly and eat dust." Then God told Eve, "You will have pain when you have a baby." God told Adam, "You must work hard to grow your food now, and one day you will die."

God made Adam and Eve leave the garden.

—based on Genesis 3

MAKE THE CONNECTION

ask what def of sin

- Adam and Eve disobeyed God and sinned against Him. To sin is to think, say, or behave in any way that goes against God and His commands. Ever since Adam and Eve sinned, all people have sinned. Because God is holy, sin has broken our relationship with God and the consequence for sin is separation from God. When our relationship with God is broken, we are defined by our sin.

- Our sin separates us from God, but God still loves us. God promised a Rescuer would come from Eve's family. God sent His Son, Jesus, to rescue people from sin and bring them back to God.

DEEPER STUDY

- Lead the group in a deeper study of being defined by sin. Explain that Genesis 3 begins by telling that the serpent was the most cunning (trickiest or most crafty) than any animal God had made. Ask kids to look in Genesis 3:1 and find out what question the serpent, who is Satan, asked Eve.

- Satan had a plan to tempt Eve to think about doing wrong. How did the woman answer the serpent in verses 2 and 3?

- Look back at Genesis 2:16-17 with the group to find out what God really said. Ask kids to identify how Eve's response was different from God's words in Genesis 2.

- Ask, "In Genesis 3:5, what did Satan say was God's reason for His instruction not to eat from the tree of the knowledge of good and evil? How was Satan tempting the woman think about doing wrong?"

- Call on a volunteer to read verse 6. Ask, "According to verse 6, why did the woman eat the fruit? Who else did she convince to eat the fruit?" Explain that after Adam and Eve sinned, changes began to happen right away. Guide kids to find Genesis 3:7 and explain what happened after Adam and Eve ate the fruit.

- Guide kids to look in verses 8 and 9 for even more changes. Explain that Adam and Eve gave excuses to God for what they had done. Ask kids to share the excuses they gave in Genesis 3:12-13? Ask, "What are some ways we make excuses for our sin?"

- Direct kids to locate Ephesians 2:1 in their Bibles and find the word dead. Explain that dead is sometimes used in the Bible to describe someone who is separated from God because of their sin.

- Turn in your Bible to Romans 6:23 and read it aloud. Help boys and girls understand that "death" includes both physical death and being separated from God because of sin.

- Explain that sin means to think, say, or behave in any way that goes against God and His commands. When we sin against God, our identity is broken by sin. We are all created in God's image, but now that image is broken by our sin and rebellion against God.

- Ask kids to identify who Paul said was dead in their sins according to Ephesians 2:1. Note that ever since Adam and Eve sinned against God, all people have sinned and are separated from God.

- Invite a volunteer to read Ephesians 2:2 Ask kids to explain what these verses mean. Identify the "ruler of the power of the air" as Satan. Explain that this verse teaches us that all people sin, including us. Before trusting in Jesus, all people are called enemies of God. We are defined by our sin and broken relationship with God.

- Recall together how the serpent, who is Satan, tempted both Adam and Eve. Adam and Eve did not trust God's plan and they disobeyed God.

- Call on another volunteer to read Ephesians 2:3. Explain that this verse tells us that just like Adam and Eve, we are sinners too. Our thoughts, words, and behaviors have gone against God and His commands. Because of our sin, we are separated from God and our identity is broken.

- That is bad news, but Paul had good news too. Read Ephesians 2:4-5. Explain that Paul wanted people to know that they could have new life by trusting in Jesus. We deserve to die because of our sin, but God loves us and keeps His promises. God sent Jesus to be our Savior. Jesus never sinned, but He died in our place. He was the sacrifice made once and for all for the forgiveness of sin (1 Peter 3:18). Jesus rose from the dead on the third day, and those who trust in Him receive forgiveness and eternal life.

MEMORIZE

Tempt Scenario

- Call attention to the "Key Passage Poster." Lead kids to read aloud the entire passage together. Challenge kids to repeat verse 10 from memory. Explain that today they will memorize verse 1. Remind kids that over the next several weeks, they will memorize all of Ephesians 2:1-10 together.

- Repeat Ephesians 2:1 together. Review the meaning of dead in the verses. Ask kids what "transgressions" or "trespasses" are (other words for sins). Emphasize that all people are broken by sin and separated from God.

- Write Ephesians 2:1 on a dry erase board or large piece of paper. Lead kids to read the verse together. Call on a volunteer to erase or cover one word of the verse. Let the group repeat the verse supplying the missing word when it is needed. Allow another volunteer to erase another word. Repeat the verse again. Continue until the entire verse is erased and kids are repeating the verse by memory.

- If time allows, repeat the activity with Ephesians 2:10 to review. Begin the passage again with kids repeating verse 1 by memory, reading verses 2-9 together, and then repeating verse 10 by memory.

PRAY

- Invite kids to close their eyes and pray silently as you pray aloud. Ask God to help kids realize when Satan is tempting them to sin. Thank Him for loving people enough to provide a way to be forgiven of their sins through Jesus.

INVESTIGATE

You Will Need:
Activity Books, pencils

Teaching Tip:
Family Guide pages are located in the back of each Activity Book. They can be printed each week from Item 2 of the downloadable printable items as needed.

- Transition kids into small groups, forming an older and younger group. If you have a large group of either older or younger kids, form groups of about 5 or 6 kids. Distribute Activity Books and pencils.

- Remind the group that each week they will have pages in the Activity Books to complete. Call attention to the puzzles and fun activities in this week's pages that can help them learn more about God and their relationship with Him.

- Review the main points from Session 1's daily pages. Lead kids to share what God taught them through their study of His Word over the last week. Praise kids for their commitment to study God's Word and encourage them to continue in their study at home. Call attention to the Family Guide pages at the back of their workbook. Encourage kids to share this page with their parents and discuss what they learned this week.

- Complete the activities for this session. As kids work, review today's Bible story and key points. Remind kids that before trusting in Jesus, our identity is broken by our sin and rebellion against God, but God made a way for our identity to be made new in Jesus.

- Encourage kids to continue their study during the coming week. Tell them that they will learn more about this new identity in the weeks to come.

Q&A

You Will Need:
Item 6: "Q&A Cards"

To Do:
Print two copies of "Q&A Cards" on different colored paper. Cut apart the "Q&A Cards" and crumple the cards into paper balls.

Teaching Tip:
If you teach a small group of children, let the kids play as one team trying to earn all the points in as short a time as possible.

For kids who are not strong readers, read the strips aloud as they are opened.

- Invite kids to play a game to review what they have learned from today's Bible study. Form two teams. Toss the paper balls onto the floor. Explain that teams will take turns trying to match a question to its answer. Point out that there are ten questions and ten answers.

- Assign each team a color corresponding to the colored paper you printed the cards on. Tell teams they will each have 30 seconds to open their team's pieces of paper and try to match as many questions and answers together as they can. If the team matches the correct questions and answers, they earn 100 points for each correct match. If the team has an incorrect match, no points are awarded. All papers on the floor should be crumpled back up for the next turn.

- Choose a team to start the game. Kids may search until they find a match or until 30 seconds expire. Keep playing until all the matches have been made.

- Call attention to the Bible references on the answer strips. Distribute the answers and let kids find the references in their Bibles. Lead kids to take turns reading their assigned verses and finding out how the Bible verse tells the answer to the question.

- Remind kids that the consequence or punishment for sin is separation from God, but God provided a plan to bring people back to Him.

THE WORD'S THE KEY

You Will Need:
Item 4: "Key Passage Poster"
Plain paper and a marker or a dry erase board, dry erase marker, and eraser

To Do:
Determine 2 or 3 key words from verses 1 and 10 of Ephesians 2. If you are using paper, print the same number of blanks as there are letters in the key word, each word on separate sheets of paper.
Make additional pages for one or two major words from most verses between 2 and 10 of chapter 2.
If you choose to use a dry erase board, draw the appropriate number of blanks each time kids will guess a new word.

Teaching Tip:
Keep a list of letters that have been guessed for a word to help kids know what letters remain to be guessed.

- Explain that memorizing Bible verses can help kids remember what they learn from the Bible. Remind kids they are memorizing Ephesians 2:1-10 during this study. Suggest they play a game to help them memorize and understand the verses they are learning.

- Lead this activity similar to hangman. Draw the number of blanks for the first key word from verse 1 or 10 you chose.

- Allow kids to take turns naming letters of the alphabet. If a child names a letter from the word, print it on all the blanks that should contain that letter. That child then has the opportunity to guess the word. If he cannot do so, play passes to the next player. Keep playing until the word is guessed or completed.

- When a word is completed, call on a child to tell what the word means. As needed, help kids understand any unfamiliar words.

- After the second word has been completed, ask kids to determine whether the second word comes before or after the first one in the Bible passage. Kids may refer to Ephesians 2 in their Bibles or to the "Key Passage Poster."

- After the third word is completed, let kids decide whether the third word goes before, after, or between the first two words. Note that not all words of the verse will be used in the game, but the main words can help them remember the message of the Bible verse.

- Continue using the key words you chose from other verses and letting kids put them in the order used in the verses.

- Lead kids to read the entire passage from the poster. Then encourage kids to repeat both verse 1 and verse 10 by memory. If needed, lead the kids to repeat the verses several times.

INCREASE

You Will Need:
Item 2: "Family Guide"
Item 4: "Key Passage Poster"
Item 7: "Clap and Stomp!"
A chair for each child and a rope

To Do:
Place chairs in a circle with the seats facing outward. Place a "Clap and Stomp!" card in each chair.

Teaching Tip:
Change the order the cards or place blank cards on the chairs after each round to make the game more challenging.

- Invite kids to play "Clap and Stomp!" Let kids place a "Clap and Stomp!" card in each chair.

- Explain that you will begin to clap a rhythm and kids will clap along with you. As they clap, guide kids to walk around the chairs in a circle. As soon as someone notices you have stopped clapping, she will stomp her foot one time, grab the card in the chair closest to her, hold it in the air and shout her name. Warn kids that things could get noisy!

- Begin clapping as kids walk, then stop clapping and let kids respond. Call on a child to read her card and provide the correct answer.

- Place all the cards back on the chairs and play again. Note that no one is ever out in this game.

- Remind the group that Paul wrote to teach people about their identity in Christ, who God says they are. Paul taught that everyone has sinned and been separated from God. To sin is to think, say, or behave in any way that goes against God and His commands.

- Before trusting in Jesus, our identity is broken by our sin against God, but the good news is that God has also made a plan so people can be forgiven of sin. Mention that kids will learn more about that part of the plan during the next session.

- Share these short phrases as a preview to the next session: God rules. We sinned. God provided. Jesus gives. We respond.

- Urge kids to be ready to learn more about these statements.

- Lead the group to read the memory passage together from the display.

- Pray, thanking God for a plan to bring people back to Him.

- Place a rope stretched out on the floor. Let kids take turns repeating the words of Ephesians 2:1 as they jump side to side over the rope. After each kid has a turn, direct the group to jump again using the words of Ephesians 2:10.

- Remind kids to complete this week's daily activities in their workbooks. Encourage kids to complete this session's "Family Guide" with an adult at home. Distribute a "Family Guide" for this week's session if needed.

Transformed by the Gospel

KEY VERSE: "YOU ARE SAVED BY GRACE THROUGH
FAITH, AND THIS IS NOT FROM YOURSELVES; IT IS GOD'S
GIFT—NOT FROM WORKS SO THAT NO ONE CAN BOAST."
EPHESIANS 2:8–9

THROUGH THIS STUDY, KIDS CAN ...

KNOW	**UNDERSTAND**	**DISCOVER**
Trusting in Jesus for salvation transforms your identity.	God's salvation is eternal. Nothing can separate believers from God's love.	God's salvation is a gift that every person needs and can receive.

INITIATE

Teaching Tip:
If you have an uneven number of kids, guide a leader to partner with a child.

WHAT'S DIFFERENT?

- Welcome kids as they arrive.

- Guide kids to partner together and determine which kid in the pair has the first birthday in the year. Instruct kids to stand back to back with their partners. Direct the kids with the first birthdays to quickly change something about their appearance. Call time after a few seconds and let kids face each other while the child who made no changes looks for the change in appearance the partner made.

- Invite kids to share the changes they found.

- Instruct kids to stand back to back again while the other partner in each pair changes his appearance. After a few seconds, direct kids to face each other. Challenge kids to find the changes.

- Guide kids to change partners and play again as time allows.

- Point out that the point of the game was "change." Remind kids that you've been studying about identity. Lead kids to review the previous two sessions (Created by God and Broken by Sin).

- Explain that during this session's study, kids will learn about a change that is more complete and more important than the changes they made during the game—this change transforms someone's identity

TRANSFORMED BY THE GOSPEL

INQUIRE

You Will Need:
Item 4: "Key Passage Poster"
Item 8: "Gospel Statements"
5 envelopes

To Do:
Display the "Key Passage Poster."

Print and cut apart the 5 "Gospel Statements." Put each statement in an envelope. Number the envelopes 1–5.

Teaching Tip:
Consider inviting a man to read the part of the story when God spoke to Saul and then to Ananias or record a man reading these parts of the story before the session. Give the reader a copy of the Bible story so he will know when to read. Position the reader behind the group or hidden in a corner out of sight but where he can easily be heard.

OPEN UP: TURN AROUND

- Lead kids to form a circle. Once in place, kids may choose to face inward, outward, to the left, or to the right.

- Cue kids to make quarter, half, or full turns using 90 degrees, 180 degrees, and 360 degrees as commands. After each turn, if kids are eye-to-eye with someone next to them or across the circle, they have successfully "made contact." Continue calling out commands. The first player to make five contacts wins.

- Explain that today's Bible story is about someone who made a complete turnaround to follow Jesus. Jesus transformed his life forever.

- Guide the kids to find Ephesians 1:1 in their Bibles. Recall together that Paul is the person who wrote the Book of Ephesians, a letter to the church at Ephesus.

- Then invite kids to find and read Acts 9:1. Explain that Saul and Paul are the same person, but that Saul started to be called Paul between the time of this Bible story and the time he wrote Ephesians.

- Challenge the kids to notice as many ways Saul changed as they can while you tell the Bible story in your own words. Note: Some kids may point out that Saul's name became Paul. Remind the group that Scripture does not indicate that Saul changed his name to Paul. Saul is the Hebrew pronunciation for this name. Paul is his Greek name.

TELL THE BIBLE STORY: SAUL'S CONVERSION

Saul was an enemy of those who believed in Jesus. Saul entered house after house and dragged the believers away to prison. He made murderous threats against Jesus' followers, requesting permission from the high priest to travel to Damascus and arrest believers there.

As Saul was nearing Damascus, a bright light from heaven flashed around him. The light blinded Saul, and he fell to the ground. He heard a voice ask: "Why are you persecuting (hurting) Me?" "Who are You, Lord?" Saul asked.

"I am Jesus, the one you are persecuting," was the answer. "Go into the city. You will be told what to do."

Saul's traveling partners led him to the city. He could not see for three days. God told a man named Ananias, "Go to Saul. He has been praying. He knows you are coming to help him see again."

Ananias replied, "Lord, I have heard how much evil this man has done." God replied, "Go because I have chosen this man to tell the Gentiles about Me!" Ananias obeyed. When he put his hands on Saul's eyes, Saul could see again. Saul was baptized and immediately began to preach in the synagogues about Jesus. "Jesus is God's Son!" Saul announced.

Some Jews were angry with Saul's new message. They plotted to kill him. Saul's friends helped him escape Damascus by lowering him over the wall in a basket. Saul went back to Jerusalem and continued to speak boldly about his faith in Jesus.

—based on Acts 9:1-20

MAKE THE CONNECTION

- Explain that Saul was originally convinced he was a blameless and law-abiding follower of God. Meeting Jesus made it clear to Saul that he was a sinner and needed forgiveness. Jesus appeared to Saul and changed him from the inside out. Jesus Christ came into the world to save sinners. (1 Tim. 1:15) Jesus called Saul, also known as Paul, who was once an enemy

(1 Tim. 1:15) Jesus called Saul, also known as Paul, who was once an enemy to Christians, to spend the rest of his life telling people the gospel and leading them to trust Jesus as Lord and Savior.

- When we trust in Jesus, we aren't just saying that we agree with the idea of Jesus as God's Son. Through the gospel, God opens our eyes to who Jesus really is. We put our trust in Him, believing that His death on the cross provides forgiveness for our sins and that because He was raised from the dead, He is King over everything. When we trust in Jesus, He changes our hearts. He removes our identity as a sinner and gives us a new identity—child of God!

DEEPER STUDY

- Mention that the word *gospel* means "good news." The gospel is the good news that God sent His Son, Jesus, into the world to rescue sinners. Distribute 5 envelopes to different children. At your prompting, guide each child to open the envelope one at a time and read the statement inside. After each statement is read, give a brief explanation of each one.

  - *1. God rules.* The Bible tells us that God created everything, and He is in charge of everything. Invite a volunteer to read Genesis 1:1 from the Bible. Read Revelation 4:11 or Colossians 1:16-17 aloud and explain what these verses mean.
  - *2. We sinned.* During the last session, we learned that everyone who has ever lived, except Jesus, has sinned. Since the time of Adam and Eve, everyone has chosen to disobey God. (Rom. 3:23) Because God is holy, God cannot be around sin. Sin separates us from God and deserves God's punishment of death. (Rom. 6:23)
  - *3. God provided.* Choose a child to read John 3:16 aloud. Say that God sent His perfect Son, Jesus, to rescue us from the punishment we deserve. It's something we, as sinners, could never earn on our own. Jesus alone saves us. God's salvation is a gift that every person needs and can receive. Read and explain Ephesians 2:8-9.
  - *4. Jesus gives.* Share with kids that Jesus lived a perfect life, died on the cross for our sins, and rose again. Because Jesus gave up His life for us, we can be welcomed into God's family for eternity. This is the best gift ever! Read Romans 5:8, 2 Corinthians 5:21, or 1 Peter 3:18.
  - *5. We respond.* Tell kids that they can respond to Jesus. Read Romans 10:9-10, 13. Review these aspects of our response: Believe in your heart that Jesus alone saves you through what He's already done on the cross. Repent, turning from self and sin to Jesus. Tell God and others that your faith is in Jesus.

- Invite kids to locate Ephesians 1:20-22. Ask which of the five "Gospel Statements" the verse relates to. *(God Rules)* Remind kids that they learned that God rules over everything. He created people in His image and has all authority to determine our identity and purpose.

- Lead kids to find Ephesians 2 in their Bibles. Ask if anyone can recite verse 1 from memory. Direct kids to read verse 1 and ask which of the five "Gospel Statements" this verse relates to. *(We sinned.)* Remind kids they learned in Session 2 that sin brings separation from God and punishment for sin. Guide the kids to read verse 3 and decide which statement it relates to. *(We sinned.)*

- Continue with verse 4 *(God provided)*, verse 5 *(Jesus gives)* and verse 10 *(We respond)*. Explain that when a person trusts Jesus as Savior, her whole identity is transformed! Offer to talk with any child who is interested in responding to Jesus.

MEMORIZE

- Call attention to the "Key Passage Poster." Point out that kids have already memorized the first and last verses of the passage. Challenge the kids to repeat those verses by memory but to read the middle verses from the poster.

- Direct attention to verses 8-9 and read them together. Point out that these verses give important information about Jesus' gift of salvation. Explain that no one can work hard enough or be good enough to be forgiven of their sins and made right with God. Show that verse 8 says "grace through faith" saves a person from their sins, and grace is a gift of God. God's salvation is a gift that every person needs and can receive. Lead the group to read the verses together several times. Challenge them to repeat as much of the two verses as they can without looking.

PRAY

- Remark that God's love for His people is amazing. State that God's salvation lasts forever because He will not let anything separate believers from His love. (Rom. 8:37-39)

- Mention that the Holy Spirit convicts people at different times when they are ready to trust Jesus as their Savior and Lord. Note that some ways they will know the Holy Spirit is helping them are that they will realize how serious their sin is (conviction), understand their separation from God and need for a Savior, and desire to turn from their sin and trust in Jesus (repentance). Comment that some kids in the group may already have trusted Jesus as their Savior, while others may be asking questions.

- Lead kids to pray silently, suggesting they either pray that God will help them know when the time is right for them to trust Jesus as Savior, or thank God that He is already their Savior and Lord. After a few moments, add a quiet "Amen."

INVESTIGATE

You Will Need:
Activity Books, pencils

- Transition kids into small groups (an older and younger group). Distribute Activity Books and pencils.

- Review the main points of Session 2's daily pages. Lead kids to share what God taught them through studying His Word. Encourage kids for their commitment to study God's Word and encourage them to continue in their study at home. Call attention to the family page for Session 3 at the back of their workbook. Encourage kids to share this page with their parents and discuss what they learned this week.

- Guide kids to complete this session's activities in their Activity Books. Review the "Digging Deeper" activity for the week and discuss what kids have learned about who they truly are.

- As kids work, review today's Bible story and key points. Remind kids that trusting in Jesus for salvation transforms their identity. Jesus changes the identity of every believer from broken by sin to child of God! When you trust in Jesus for salvation, your identity is in Christ—who God says you are.

- Encourage kids to continue their study during the coming week. Tell them that they will learn more about this new identity in the weeks to come.

MIX AND MATCH WALL DISPLAY

You Will Need:
Item 9: "Mix and Match"
Gift bag, yarn, tape, and scissors

To Do:
Cut apart the "Mix and Match" cards. Place the word cards in the gift bag.

Teaching Tip:
If you cannot put tape on the wall, use a bulletin board or provide a large sheet of cardboard.

- Suggest kids create a wall display of important words often used to help a person understand how to be saved. Explain that being saved is another way of saying "become a Christian."

- Invite a volunteer to remove a word card from the bag and read the word aloud. Choose another volunteer to read the definition card that matches the chosen word. Place the two cards where kids can see the match. Continue until each card in the bag has been matched to a definition card.

- Instruct the kids to mix the word cards and work together taping the cards to the wall in a column. Kids then mix the definition cards and tape them to the wall in mixed up order across from the first column.

- Call for a kid to choose one word from the first column and decide which card is the definition of the word. If he is correct, he uses a piece of yarn and tape to connect the two cards. If he is not correct, other kids may give him clues to find the right definition before he uses the yarn to connect the two. Continue with the other cards.

- If time allows, mix both sets of cards on the wall again. Work together to match the words and definitions.

- Point out that trusting in Jesus for salvation transforms someone's identity because he is forgiven of sin and adopted into God's family.

MEMORY VERSE SAND ART

You Will Need:
Item 4: "Key Passage Poster"
A small, empty bottle with a lid for each child; small funnels (or paper to use as funnels); index cards; different colors of sand; pens or thin markers; tape

To Do:
If you don't have colored sand available, you can make your own "sand" by crushing colored chalk and mixing it with salt.

Teaching Tip:
Urge kids not to mix their sand colors too much. Too much stirring can make the sand all one color instead of showcasing the beautiful colors.

- Lead kids to read the entire memory passage together from the poster. Call for kids who can repeat Ephesians 2:1 from memory to do so. Continue by letting kids who can repeat verse 10 from memory do so. Challenge kids to repeat verses 8-9 from memory, but offer help as needed. Emphasize that God's salvation is a gift that every person needs and can receive.

- Suggest the group make sand art gifts for their families that will help them know about God's wonderful gift of salvation. Distribute the cards and let kids print the words of Ephesians 2:8-9 on them. Explain that the cards can be taped to the sand art gifts.

- Give each kid an empty bottle. Tell the kids they can layer the sand into the bottles in any order they want to create their unique designs. Demonstrate adding sand with a funnel. Kids may add special effects to their designs by poking a toothpick or drinking straw inside of the bottle to gently stir a layer of sand.

- As kids work, review Ephesians 2:8-9 and ask kids to explain its meaning. Encourage the group to share their sand art with their families but also share the Bible verses they have memorized. Let kids attach the key verse cards to their sand art.

- Direct the kids to hold their sand art bottles and repeat Ephesians 2:8-9, remembering that God's salvation is a gift that every person needs and can receive.

INCREASE

You Will Need:
Item 2: "Family Guide"
Item 3: "Allergy Alert Poster"
Item 4: "Key Passage Poster"
Item 10: "Ephesians 2:8-9 Cards"
2 clear containers, instant fruit drink mix, water, spoons, baking soda, vinegar, dry tissue

Teaching Tips:
If you teach a large group of children, consider forming two groups who do the same experiment so that all kids can be close enough to see the transformation in the liquids.

Use a large work space to conduct this experiment.

- Show the drink mix and the water. Ask kids what will happen when the two are mixed together. After responses, call on a volunteer to pour the drink mix into the water. Let another kid stir the two together. Ask whether kids predicted correctly.

- Show the baking soda and vinegar. Ask kids what will happen when these two are mixed together. Call on a child to pour the vinegar over the baking soda using a different container.

- Ask whether anyone in the group can turn the drink mixture back into two separate ingredients, water and drink mix. Invite kids to think about ways they might separate the baking soda and vinegar. Note for kids that the combinations cannot be separated again, just like people who become part of God's family can never be separated from God's family. Remark that God has adopted everyone who trusts in Jesus as their Savior into His family and He will never turn them away.

- Instruct the group to stand. Spread the word cards from today's memory verses on the floor. Hold a tissue in your hand with your arm straight out. Explain that you will release the tissue, and when it hits the floor, everyone must grab one or two cards until all the cards are taken.

- The group will take turns reading their words in the order of the verses. Kids may refer to the "Key Passage Poster" as needed. Collect the cards and play again. After several rounds, remove the poster and play the game again.

- Encourage kids to complete this session's "Family Guide" with an adult at home. Distribute a "Family Guide" for this week's session if needed.

- Conclude this session's activities as you remind kids of the daily Bible study pages in the Activity Books. Challenge kids to use the pages daily to help them know more about their relationship with God.

Who We Are in Christ

KEY VERSE: "BUT GOD, WHO IS RICH IN MERCY, BECAUSE OF HIS GREAT LOVE THAT HE HAD FOR US, MADE US ALIVE WITH CHRIST EVEN THOUGH WE WERE DEAD IN TRESPASSES. YOU ARE SAVED BY GRACE!"
EPHESIANS 2:4–5

THROUGH THIS STUDY, KIDS CAN ...

KNOW

You are who God says you are

UNDERSTAND

Everyone who trusts in Jesus receives a new identity.

DISCOVER

God defines the true identity of all followers of Jesus.

INITIATE

You Will Need:
Item 3: "Allergy Alert Poster"
Item 11: "Human Vine Assignments"
Masking tape, grapes
For each team of 4: Bible, cotton balls, spoon, bowl, and cup

To Do:
Post the Allergy Alert listing the grapes. Tape a starting line on the floor. For each team (vine) of 4 kids, number a set of assignment cards. Place each assignment card and any materials needed for it in random places around the room. (The further apart, the more fun!)

Teaching Tip:
For older kids, consider forming vines of girls only and vines of boys only.

For smaller groups, consider making one vine and let kids race the clock to complete the assignments.

HUMAN VINE

- Welcome kids to the group. Form teams of four. Instruct the team members to line up at the tape line and join hands with the person behind them. The leader can keep one hand free. The last kid in line will use both his hands to hold the hand of the player before him.

- Explain that teams must move as a "vine" without dropping hands. Mention that if a vine drops hands at any point, they must return to the beginning and start again. Point out the different stations. Tell the players the vine leader (the one with a free hand) will lead the vine to a station and must complete the assignment on the card using only her free hand. Note that kids can move to different stations in any order, so long as they complete all four stations. Once the first player completes the assignment, he moves to the back of the vine and joins hands with the person in front of him. The new leader guides the vine to the next station. The winner of the game is the first vine (team) to complete all four assignments and return to the start line.

- After the game is played, distribute grapes first to the winning vine, then to other vines. As they eat, remind kids that they have been learning about their identity in Christ—who God says they are.

- Review the main points of the last few sessions:

  - God created people in His image and for His glory. He has the authority to determine our identity and purpose.
  - Before trusting Jesus, our identity is broken by our sin and rebellion against God.
  - Trusting in Jesus for salvation transforms our identity. God's salvation is a gift that every person needs and can receive.

- Remark that today's Bible story is about a time Jesus used a vine to teach His disciples about their identity as believers—who God says they are.

INQUIRE

You Will Need:
Item 4: "Key Passage Poster"
A grape vine (a real or artificial grape vine, an ivy plant, or a vine you make from twisted paper and flat leaves), sheets of paper, markers, world map or globe

Teaching Tip:
Be attentive to helping kids understand more than the literal information about tending vines.

OPEN UP: LEARN ABOUT VINES

- Mention that fruit was a big part of agriculture in Jesus' day. Show your vine and explain that Jesus used a grapevine in today's Bible story to teach His followers about their identity as disciples.

- Pass the vine from person to person as you present these additional facts about growing fruit on vines:

  - Fruit grows best when planted on hillsides where they can have sunlight from above and water from rain that runs off the hill.
  - Vines often need to be pruned, or cut back, during the winter.
  - Pruning means to cut off the dead branches and leave the healthy branches to grow and produce fruit.
  - During the harvest time, the farmer's family might have lived out in the field where they could keep robbers from stealing the fruit at night.
  - During the day, the family picked the fruit.

- Suggest the kids keep these facts in mind as they listen to today's Bible story from John.

- Open your Bible to John 15. Place the vine before the group. Tell the following Bible story in your own words.

TELL THE BIBLE STORY: THE VINE AND THE BRANCHES

Jesus said, "I am the true vine. My Father is the gardener. The gardener cuts off every branch in Me that does not produce fruit. However, if a branch is producing fruit, He prunes it (cuts off just the dead parts) so the branch can continue to produce fruit."

Then Jesus reminded His disciples they are already followers of Him. Jesus told His disciples He wanted them to remain in Him, just like a healthy branch produces fruit when it stays attached to the vine. He explained that He would remain in them, too. He pointed out that a branch broken off the vine cannot produce any fruit but must stay connected to the vine in order to produce fruit.

Again, Jesus repeated, "I am the vine" This time, however, He added that His followers were the branches. He urged them to remain in Him in order to produce much fruit. He said, "Without Me, you can do nothing. If you don't remain in Me, you are like one of the branches that is carried off to be burned up."

Jesus encouraged the believers to remain in Him and in His words. "God is glorified when you produce much fruit and show that you are My disciples," Jesus said.

— based on John 15:1-8

MAKE THE CONNECTION

- God defines the true identity of all followers of Jesus. When we trust in Jesus for salvation, our identity (who we are) is changed and transformed by the gospel. Jesus shared this story with His disciples to teach them what it means to grow as a disciple. Tell kids that "producing fruit" refers to growing to look more like Jesus and caring about the things Jesus cares about.

- Like fruit grows when it is connected to the vine, Christians grow to look more like Jesus when we are connected to Him. Everyone who trusts in Jesus receives a new identity. Jesus rescues us from sin and frees us to live a life that honors God. We are in the process of becoming who we really are—who God says we are. By doing what is good and right, people who trust Jesus can show that they really believe in Him.

DEEPER STUDY

- Direct kids to open their Bibles to John 15:1. Lead a volunteer to read the verse aloud. Ask the group to identify who the true vine is and who the gardener is in this verse.

- Lead kids to read John 15:5 aloud. Ask kids to identify who Jesus describes here as the vine and branches.

- Mention that Jesus was talking to people who already trusted in Him as Savior. He told them this parable or story about the vine and branches to help them understand that they are now transformed, or changed because they trust in Jesus. He didn't mean that their hair color changed or they got taller. Jesus referred to their hearts changing—their identity.

- Instruct kids to turn in their Bibles to Ephesians 1:5. Read the verse aloud. Point out the word "adopted" in the verse. Explain that when a person trusts Jesus as Savior and Lord, he is adopted. Adoption is when God welcomes us into His family as His children.

- Assist kids in finding Acts 10:43 and identifying another way believers are changed. *(Changed from sinful to forgiven)*

- Continue by locating Romans 8:5 and discovering another way believers are different. *(Minds set on the things of the Spirit)*

- Guide kids to read James 1:22 and to find another change for believers from unbelievers. *(Obedience to God)*

- Explain that everyone who trusts in Jesus receives a new identity, but that new identity won't be fully complete until Jesus returns and makes us sinless like Him. Until then, Christians continue growing to look more like Jesus. This means we are in the process of becoming who we really are—who God defines us to be.

- Jesus taught that we can live out our identity as Christians by remaining or abiding in Him. Trusting in Jesus frees us to live a life that honors God. By obeying God's Word, saying no to sin with the help of the Holy Spirit, and loving others like Jesus loves we can show others that we really believe in Him.

MEMORIZE

- Lead the group to read the entire key passage from the "Key Passage Poster." Call for volunteers to take turns repeating key passage verses from memory without looking at the poster.

- Suggest the group focus on memorizing verses 4 and 5 today. Assign various kids to print different phrases of the verses on sheets of paper. For example, "his great love," "rich in mercy," "alive with Christ," "by grace," and "have been saved." (Use other similar phrases if you are memorizing a different translation.)

● Spread the pages in random order and tape them to the floor. Keep the "Key Passage Poster" displayed. Let kids take turns repeating the words of the verse in order as they jump to the appropriate paper until they reach the end of the verse. Let kids take several turns as time allows.

● Lead the group to repeat the entire passage without looking at the poster for the verses they have already learned.

PRAY

● Show a world map or globe. Remark that God defines the true identity of all followers of Jesus, no matter where in the world they are.

● Invite kids to look at the map and pick a particular country. Then ask them to pray silently, asking God to help believers in that country tell others about Him. Then ask kids to focus on their own town. Encourage them to continue to pray silently, asking God to help your church and other believers in their towns tell about Jesus. After a few moments, add "Amen."

INVESTIGATE

You Will Need:
Activity Books, pencils

Teaching Tip:
To help kids remember to bring their Activity Books to each session post a reminder on social media or send parents a text message, email, or make a phone call during the week to remind them.

- Transition kids into small groups, forming an older group and a younger group. If you have a large group of either older or younger kids, form groups of about 5 or 6 kids. Distribute the Activity Books and pencils.

- Complete this session's Activity Book pages together with your group, being sensitive to questions and levels of understanding.

- As kids work, review today's Bible story and what it means to grow to look more like Jesus. Point out the pages for kids to complete at home. Explain that working on the pages can help them learn more about who God says they are in Christ. Encourage kids to continue their study during the coming week.

- Encourage kids to complete "Digging Deeper" in their Activity Books.

PLAY A SPEED STACK GAME TO LEARN MEMORY VERSES

You Will Need:
Item 4: "Key Passage Poster"
Item 12: "Speed Stack Memory Verse Strips" (one copy for each team)
10 plastic cups for each team, scissors, and tape

To Do:
Cut apart the memory verse strips.

Teaching Tip:
Consider letting an early arriver cut the strips apart before the session begins.

- Challenge teams to find how quickly they can stack their cups into a pyramid using these instructions: The pyramids will have four cups on the bottom, three on the next row, two on the next, and one on top. Each person on the team must stack at least one cup during the game. The first team to correctly stack its cups wins.

- Give a signal to begin and let teams work. Announce the winning team. Suggest kids unstack the cups and play the game again. Praise kids for following the rules as they play.

- Tell kids the game will now get more difficult. Distribute ten paper strips to each team and let kids tape each strip to a different cup.

- Explain that kids will now make their pyramids in the same way, except that the Bible verse must be in reading order. The winner will be the first team to read aloud their verse in order. Once kids have their cups labeled, give the signal to begin the game. If teams have difficulty remembering the order of the verses, they may look in a Bible or at the "Key Passage Poster" for help.

- Play the game several times, urging teams to go faster each time.

- End by leading the group to repeat the verses together and then to repeat the entire key passage together.

WHO WE ARE IN CHRIST

MAKE BALLOON DISPLAYS

You Will Need:
Item 13: "Balloon Display"
Several inflated balloons, a large trash bag, permanent markers, string or ribbon, tape

To Do:
Tie a string or ribbon to each balloon. Put the balloons in the trash bag until needed.

Teaching Tip:
Before the session, scout the church for likely places for kids to display their balloons. Decide whether permission is needed for any of the places.

- Review with kids what Jesus taught using the vine as an example. (*Jesus is the vine; God is the gardener; believers in Jesus are the branches; believers must stay with Jesus to grow in their faith and look more like Him*)

- Invite a child to choose a "Balloon Display" card for all kids to find in the Bible. Call on a child to read the verse. Ask the kids to tell what they find about the identity of believers in Jesus. Ask a volunteer to print the answer on a balloon. Let another child make a tape loop and stick the balloon to a wall or door.

- Distribute other Bible reference cards and let kids determine more traits of believers in Jesus. For each one, let one kid print the answer on a balloon and let another kid tape the balloon to the wall. Call on a child to print *A believer is...* on another balloon, then add it to the display.

- Suggest kids share what they have learned by spreading their displays out to other locations. Let each kid print "A believer is" on a balloon and then choose one of the attributes of believers to print on another balloon. When kids have two balloons ready, let them go to different locations in the hallway or other parts of the building and tape their two balloons on door frames, empty bulletin boards, or other appropriate places.

- Gather in the classroom again. Remind kids that a believer's identity is who God says she is. Explain that until Jesus returns and makes all things new, we will continue to sin, but we are in the process of becoming who we really are—who God says we are.

- Guide kids to pray that people will see their displays and learn more about what being a believer in Jesus (or Christian) means for them.

INCREASE

You Will Need:
Item 2: "Family Guide"
Item 4: "Key Passage Poster"
Item 14: "The Vine"
Paper plates used earlier in the session

To Do:
Print and cut apart "The Vine" leaves. Display the "Key Passage Poster."

- Continue reviewing today's Bible material with a game where kids work as one big group to guess words from the Bible story.

- Invite a volunteer to choose one of "The Vine" cards, then act out one letter at a time without speaking, somewhat like charades. They can try to make the shape of the letter with their hands or body, or act out something that begins with that letter. (Example: Golf= G)

- Explain that when a team member guesses the word, the group earns 200 points. However, if the player can tell how the word was important to the story, the group earns an additional 300 points. Challenge the group to earn as many points as possible. Continue with all "The Vine" cards.

- Emphasize that Jesus wants believers to remain close to Him in their thoughts and actions. Remind kids that remaining close to Jesus and growing as a Christian involves learning and obeying God's Word, praying, and spending time thinking about God as well as telling others about Him.

- Encourage kids to each think of a way they want to grow closer to God this week. Mention they might choose to read the Bible more, to pray more, or to talk to someone about Jesus. After a few moments, pray aloud that the kids will grow closer to God through the actions they chose. Ask God to help kids do the actions they chose at the right time for them. Thank God that He wants people to grow closer to Him.

- Remind kids to complete this week's activity pages in the Activity Books. Remind kids to complete this session's "Family Guide" with an adult at home and distribute a "Family Guide" for this week's session if needed.

▪ Lead the group to read the "Key Passage Poster" together, repeating any verses from memory when they can. Gather the paper plates used during Bible study and secure them to the floor. Let kids take turns jumping the verses again.

SESSION 5

What We Have in Christ

KEY VERSE: "GOD RAISED US UP WITH CHRIST AND SEATED US WITH HIM IN THE HEAVENLY REALMS IN CHRIST JESUS IN ORDER THAT IN THE COMING AGES HE MIGHT SHOW THE INCOMPARABLE RICHES OF HIS GRACE, EXPRESSED IN HIS KINDNESS TO US IN CHRIST JESUS."
EPHESIANS 2:6–7

THROUGH THIS STUDY, KIDS CAN ...

KNOW

When we trust in Jesus, God adopts us and welcomes us into His family as His children.

UNDERSTAND

Jesus came to seek and to save the lost.

DISCOVER

We receive the blessing of eternal life as an inheritance from God.

INITIATE

You Will Need:
Item 15: "Lost Things Pictures"

To Do:
Print and cut apart the "Lost Things Pictures." Use the pictures again as you tell the Bible story.

Teaching Tip:
If a second adult is unavailable to accompany the child to the hallway, ask the kid who will find the picture to stand with his back turned, cover his ears, and hum while the group hides the picture.

LOST THINGS FOUND

- Welcome kids as they arrive. Invite kids to play a game in which they take turns hunting for hidden items.

- Call on a child to step just outside the door along with another teacher. Once the child is out of the room, urge the kids to be as quiet as possible as they decide where to hide the first picture.

- After the picture is hidden, call the child back into the room. Explain that as she hunts for the picture, the rest of the group will help her by humming softly when she is far from the picture and humming louder as she gets closer and closer to the picture.

- When the first picture has been found, let the child who found it show it to the other kids in the group.

- Call for another child to step outside the door with a teacher. Remind the other kids to quietly choose where to hide the next picture. Continue as before. If time allows, keep hiding the same pictures while rotating the one to hunt the pictures.

- Explain that in today's Bible story some things were not hidden but lost, and someone was looking for them.

WHAT WE HAVE IN CHRIST

INQUIRE

You Will Need:
Item 4: "Key Passage Poster"
Item 15: "Lost Things Pictures"
Item 16: "Spiritual Blessings"
Item 17: "Prayer Sheet"
Tape, sheets of paper, and a marker

To Do:
Gather the "Lost Things Pictures" from Inquire and use as you share the Bible story. Print "Spiritual Blessings" and use during Deeper Study. Print 4 copies of "Prayer Sheet" and use as directed during the prayer time.

Teaching Tip:
If you teach mostly older kids, change the action for each response. For example, stand on your left foot for one choice and on your right foot for another choice. Or touch your ears for one choice and touch your chin for another. Keep them guessing what the next actions will be!

OPEN UP: THUMBS UP! THUMBS DOWN!

- Ask the boys and girls to show thumbs up if they have ever lost anything, or show thumbs down if they have never lost anything. Call on two or three kids to tell something they have lost.

- Ask kids to show thumbs up if losing their items felt good or thumbs down if they felt bad about it. Allow a few kids to tell how they felt. Then ask kids to show with their thumbs how they felt when the item was found or to show thumbs sideways if the item was never found. Talk about how it feels to find lost things.

- Challenge kids to notice three different things that were lost in today's Bible story and how the people who lost them felt.

- Open your Bible to Luke 15 as you tell the following Bible story in your own words. Be ready to show the appropriate picture with each segment of the story.

TELL THE BIBLE STORY: JESUS TAUGHT THREE PARABLES

Tax collectors and sinners came to listen to Jesus teach. The religious leaders complained because Jesus welcomed sinners, so Jesus told them three parables to teach them about God.

(Show the picture of the sheep.) Jesus said, "If a man has 100 sheep and loses one, what does he do? He leaves the 99 sheep in the open field and searches for the lost sheep until he finds it. Then he tells his friends, 'Let's celebrate! I found my lost sheep!' " Then Jesus said, "This is what heaven is like; there is more joy in heaven when one sinner repents and turns back to God than for 99 people who did not wander off."

(Show the picture of the coin.) Jesus said, "If a woman has 10 silver coins and loses one of them, what does she do? She lights a lamp, sweeps the house, and searches carefully until she finds it! Then she tells her friends, 'Let's celebrate! I found my lost coin!' " Then Jesus said, "This is what heaven is like. There is joy in heaven when one sinner repents and turns back to God."

(Show the picture of the son.) Finally, Jesus said, "A man had two sons. The younger son said, 'Father, give me my inheritance today.' So the father gave his son his share. The younger son left home. He wasted his money and lived foolishly. There was a famine, and the people there did not have enough food. The son got a job feeding pigs. He was so hungry, even the pigs' food looked tasty.

The younger son made a plan. He would go back to his father and admit he was wrong. He would ask to work for his father like the servants.

So the younger son headed home. He was still a long way away when his father saw him coming. His father ran to him, threw his arms around him, and kissed him. The son began to apologize. 'I have sinned against God and against you,' he said.

But the father told his servants, 'Let's celebrate with a feast! Bring the best robe and put it on my son! Put a ring on his finger and sandals on his feet. This son of mine was lost, and now he is found!'

At this time, the older son came from the fields and heard music at the house. 'What's going on?' he asked one of the servants.

'Your brother is here,' the servant said. 'Your father is celebrating.' The older brother was angry! He refused to go to the feast. The father asked him to come inside. 'Look!' the older brother said. 'I never disobeyed you! But you never threw a party for me.'

'Son,' the father said, 'everything I have is yours. We have to celebrate and be happy. Your brother was lost and is found.' "

— based on Luke 15

MAKE THE CONNECTION

- The religious leaders complained that Jesus welcomed sinners. Jesus told these parables to teach about God's forgiveness. God sent Jesus so sinners can be forgiven. As Savior, Jesus seeks sinners. He paid the ultimate price—His own life—to save people from sin.

- Jesus came to seek and save the lost. Explain that people sometimes use the word lost to describe people whose identity is broken by sin and without God, those who have not trusted Jesus as their Savior. Jesus taught people that He came to save people from their sins. Just like people are happy when something lost is found, all of heaven is happy when a person turns from sin to trusting in Jesus.

DEEPER STUDY

- Guide kids to locate Ephesians 1 in their Bibles. Remind kids that they've been learning about their identity in Christ—who God says they are—through this study. Earlier they learned about *who* people are in Christ once they have trusted Him as Savior. Note for them that in this session they can learn about *what* they have in Christ once they have trusted Him as Savior.

- Direct kids to Ephesians 1:3. Call on a volunteer to read the verse aloud. Ask kids to tell what the verse mentions that God gives to believers. Invite a child to post the "Spiritual Blessings" sign to the wall.

- Mention that the next verses in Ephesians 1 tell what some of the spiritual blessings we have in Christ are. Lead kids to verse 5 and ask them to find *adopt* or *adoption*. Remind them they learned in the last session about God adopting them into His family as His children. Call on a volunteer to add *adoption* to the wall display.

- Kids continue to verse 7 to find the word redemption. Explain that *redemption* means to pay a price to get something back from someone else. Jesus died on the cross as our substitute, taking the consequences for our sin so that we can live forever with Him. Let a child place the *redemption* sign on the wall. Also in verse 7, kids can locate the word *forgiveness* and add that to the sign.

- Instruct kids to find in verse 8 the words *wisdom* and *understanding*. Let volunteers add these words to the display. End with helping kids find *Holy Spirit* in verse 13.

- Point to the display and re-read the spiritual gifts, explaining that these are some of the gifts people have in Christ after they trust Him as Savior and Lord.

- Guide the kids to find John 3:16 in their Bibles. After a child reads the verse or repeats it from memory, point out that believers receive the blessing of eternal life as part of their inheritance from God. When you trust in Jesus for salvation, all of these things are true of who you are because God says they are true of you.

MEMORIZE

- Call attention to the "Key Passage Poster." Remark that kids have worked to learn verse 1, verses 4-5, and verses 8-10. Read verses 8-10 together one time. Then challenge the kids to repeat together all of those verses from memory. Practice a few more times.

- Suggest the group learn verses 6-7 during this session in their quest to memorize the entire passage by the end of the study. Point out that doing various actions for different words can help people remember verses. Call attention to the words *raised* and *seated* in verse 6 that could be acted out. Mention that kids might use sign language when they say "Jesus." Practice verse 6 a few times with the actions kids chose.

- Suggest kids learn verse 7 by picking a few important words in order. For example: *ages, display, riches, grace, kindness*, and *Christ Jesus*. Kids can learn the phrases that go with each key word and put them together. Practice verse 7 several times. Then lead the group to repeat both verses.

PRAY

- Show the prayer sheet. Note for kids that thinking about who God says we are and the blessings He provides can make us feel thankful for all things God has given us.

- Ask kids to take turns telling things they are thankful to God for. Print two or three responses per sheet of paper until you have completed several sheets. Encourage kids to help you tape the various papers to different areas in the room.

- Explain that kids can use the prayer chart as they pray today. Lead each child to walk to different sheets and spend time thanking God for the different responses listed. Encourage them to add their responses to the sheet if they like.

- Lead the group to quietly walk around the room and pray at each prayer sheet. End with "Amen."

INVESTIGATE

You Will Need:
Activity Books, pencils

- Transition kids into small groups, forming an older and younger group. If you have a large group of either older or younger kids, form groups of about 5 or 6 kids. Distribute the Activity Books and pencils.

- Complete the activity book pages for this session. As kids work, talk with them about today's Bible story and about what believers have in Christ.

- Point out the pages for kids to complete at home. Explain that working on the pages can help them learn more. Encourage kids to continue their study during the coming week.

PLAY "HOW'S YOUR MEMORY?"

You Will Need:
Item 4: "Key Passage Poster"
Item 18: "How's Your Memory?"
Scissors

To Do:
Post the "Key Passage Poster" where kids can refer to it during the game. Print 2 copies of "How's Your Memory?" on cardstock or heavy paper. Cut apart the cards and clip each set separately.

Teaching Tip:
If you teach a small group, challenge the kids to work together to see how few turns it takes to complete the verse. Then challenge them to beat that number as they play again.

- Suggest the group play a memory game to help them continue learning Ephesians 2:6-7.

- Form two teams. Give each team a set of "How's Your Memory?" cards. Direct each team to spread out the cards printed side down in random order. Instruct teams to mix their cards again and to change places so that each team is sitting beside the opposite set of cards.

- Explain that teams will take turns choosing one card at a time until the card with a 1 and the beginning of Ephesians 2:6 is found. That card is left with the print face up.

- During that team's next turn, the team repeats the words on the first card and chooses a new card to turn over. If that card has a 2, the team keeps the card turned right side up. If the team turns over a different card, it is turned back over and the other team takes a turn. From that point, on a team's turn, the team must repeat the words on the first cards in order before choosing a new card.

- If the next card is revealed in order, it is left face up. If not, the card is turned back over and play moves to the other team. The first team to turn over all its cards is the winner.

- If time allows, remix teams and cards before playing another round of the game.

MAKE A "WHAT WE HAVE IN CHRIST" WREATH

You Will Need:
Item 16: "Spiritual Blessings"
12 5-by-6-inch pieces of cardstock, tape, pens or thin markers, a 10-inch cardboard circle (poster board is fine), four-inch circle, aluminum foil, permanent marker, yarn or string

Teaching Tip:
Older kids can make the wreath more easily using double sided tape. Younger kids work more easily with regular tape and more supervision.

- Use the "Spiritual Blessings" strips from earlier in the session to help kids review what people have in Christ once they become believers in Jesus as Savior.

- Suggest the group make a special wreath to help others know what they can have in Jesus Christ when they believe in Him. Point out that the wreath will list eight things believers have in Christ. Guide kids to work together to make twelve paper cones. Kids may want to work together with one kid holding the rolled paper while the other kid tapes the seam.

- Assign each of these to children to print near the large point of their cones: *salvation, knowledge of Christ, Holy Spirit, promise of eternal life, adoption into God's family, forgiveness, wisdom, peace.* Call for volunteers to write on four other cones the name *Christ Jesus.*

- Assist kids in placing a long tape loop or a length of double-sided tape on the back of each cone.

- Explain that the wreath will be assembled by placing a cone on the cardboard circle at what would be 12:00 on a clock, with the small point in the center of the circle. Note for kids that the second cone is placed at what would be 3:00 on a clock, the next at 6:00, and the next at 9:00.

- Once those are in place, kids may add two cones between each of the numbers already on the cardboard. Ask a volunteer to cover the cardboard circle with foil and another kid to print *What Believers Have in Jesus* using a permanent marker. Another child can gently tape the circle to the center of the wreath. Use the string to make a hanger if desired, or just tape the wreath to a wall.

- Review together what believers in Jesus have as part of their new identity in Christ. Suggest the group display the wreath in the room so that others can read it and know what they have learned.

- Lead the group in prayer thanking God for who He says we are through Jesus. Ask God to help others who read the wreath know more about what believers have in Jesus.

INCREASE

You Will Need:
Item 2: "Family Guide"
Item 18: "How's Your Memory?"
A large glove such as a gardening glove or a baseball glove and a timer

Teaching Tip:
Be sure kids know they are talking to God as they participate in the prayer activity. Remind them that people can pray in many different ways.

- Lead kids to stand in a circle facing inward. Explain that you will set a timer for a few seconds as kids pass the glove from person to person. The person who has the glove when the timer goes off gets to tell a fact from today's Bible story or tell something believers have in Jesus.

- Hand the glove to a child, then remark that kids must pass the glove by putting it on the hand of the person beside them. That child will then remove it and put it on the hand of the person next to him, and so on. Remind kids that they must keep passing the glove until the timer goes off. Set the timer for ten seconds or so.

- Begin the game. When the timer sounds, let the child with the glove respond by telling a Bible story fact or something believers have in Jesus. Reset the timer for a different amount of time and begin again. Continue in this way for several rounds of play.

- Commend kids for what they have learned.

- Invite the kids to turn so they are standing facing the outside of the circle. Explain that today's prayer time involves kids following directions with their bodies as well as praying silently to God. Give these directions as kids respond:

  - Take 1 step forward. Thank God that He created you in the way He did.
  - Turn to your right. Ask God to help the person in front of you know more about Him.
  - Turn to the left and look up. Ask God to help you remember that He is in control and that He loves you.
  - Turn left again. Ask God to take care of the person in front of you.
  - Kneel down and say "Amen."

- Direct the kids to put the "How's Your Memory?" cards in order of Ephesians 2:6-7. Call on a volunteer to remove one of the cards. Lead kids to repeat the two verses, filling in the missing words from memory as they say the verse aloud. Ask a kid to remove another card. Lead kids to repeat the verses, filling in all the missing words. Continue until no word cards are left to be removed.

- Remind kids to complete this week's daily Bible studies in the Younger or Older Kids Activity Books. Encourage kids to complete this session's "Family Guide" in their Activity Books with an adult at home. Distribute a "Family Guide" for this week's session if needed.

NEW LIFE

OLD LIFE

Living Out Our Identity

KEY VERSE: "IN WHICH YOU PREVIOUSLY LIVED ACCORDING TO THE WAYS OF THIS WORLD, ACCORDING TO THE RULER OF THE POWER OF THE AIR, THE SPIRIT NOW WORKING IN THE DISOBEDIENT. WE TOO ALL PREVIOUSLY LIVED AMONG THEM IN OUR FLESHLY DESIRES, CARRYING OUT THE INCLINATIONS OF OUR FLESH AND THOUGHTS, AND WE WERE BY NATURE CHILDREN UNDER WRATH AS THE OTHERS WERE ALSO.
EPHESIANS 2:2–3

THROUGH THIS STUDY, KIDS CAN ...

KNOW	UNDERSTAND	DISCOVER
We are responsible for our choices.	Christians still sin because we have hearts that want to sin, but we can say no to sin by asking God for help.	As disciples, we grow in our faith and knowledge of Jesus.

INITIATE

Teaching Tip:
The trick to this activity is to keep it moving. The faster, the better! If any kids don't yet know their right from their left, put a piece of tape on the child's right hand.

RIGHT, LEFT

- Welcome kids as they arrive. Instruct kids to stand facing you, about an arm's width from each other.

- Explain that you will call out either right or left, and kids will turn that direction as quickly as they can. At first, alternate calling left and right, but gradually speed up the calling. Then begin calling either left or right at least two times in a row. Call out directions as fast as kids can follow them.

- Increase difficulty by leading kids to jog in place, stand on one foot, and so forth while they make the directed right or left turns.

- Comment that some people think the Bible is mostly just rules about what to do and what not to do. While there certainly are instructions about how to live, the Bible is not just a list of rules God wants us to follow.

- Mention that we have been studying what the Bible says about our identity—who we are in Christ. The Book of Ephesians, like most of Paul's letters, begins with a reminder of the gospel before giving instructions about how to live. This helps us remember that God's love for us is what causes our obedience. The gospel transforms us from the inside out. Our minds and hearts change to understand God better and love Him more, and then our behavior changes because of our new thoughts and new desires.

LIVING OUT OUR IDENTITY

INQUIRE

You Will Need:
Item 4: "Key Passage Poster"
Item 19: "Peter Did"
Item 20: "Prayer Posters"
Tape and markers

To Do:
Display each of the "Peter Did" statements on a different wall.
Post each "Prayer Poster" in a different part of the room. Place a marker with each sheet.

Teaching Tip:
If you teach younger kids or very active kids, tell each part of the Bible story in a different part of the room with the kids either standing to listen or sitting on the floor.

OPEN UP: RIGHT, LEFT REMIX

- Comment that today's Bible story is about Peter, one of Jesus' disciples. Explain that the group will examine Peter's life to learn about living out their identity as followers of Jesus.

- Direct kids to play the "Right, Left" game once more to find out some facts about Peter. Give turn directions until kids face one of the "Peter Did" posters. Call on a volunteer to read the poster. Give directions for kids to turn so they face another poster. Continue until all the posters have been faced and read. Urge the kids to listen and find out more about the disciple Peter.

- Open your Bible to Luke 22 as you tell the following Bible story in your own words.

TELL THE BIBLE STORY: PETER DENIED JESUS AND WAS FORGIVEN

On the night before Jesus was crucified, Peter shared the Passover supper with Jesus and the other disciples. Jesus said, "Peter, look out. Satan will test you, but I prayed that your faith will not fail." Jesus encouraged Peter to come back to the disciples after Satan tested him and help them grow strong and stay true to Jesus.

Peter didn't understand what Jesus meant. "Lord, I am ready to go with you even to prison or to die."Jesus said, "Peter, before the rooster crows today, you will deny three times that you know Me."

Later that night, Jesus was arrested. Peter followed at a distance. In the courtyard a servant saw Peter and said, "This man was with Jesus." Peter responded, "I don't know Him!"

Someone else came and said, "You are one of His followers!" Peter said, "No, I am not!"

About an hour later, a third person insisted, "He is from Galilee. He was with Jesus." Again Peter said, "I don't know what you are talking about!" Just then, the rooster crowed and Jesus turned to look at Peter. Peter remembered Jesus' words to him, "Before the rooster crows today, you will deny my three times." Peter hurried away; he wept bitterly over what he had done.

After Jesus died and rose from the dead, Jesus revealed Himself to His disciples. Peter and some of the other disciples were fishing. They had not caught any fish all night long. At sunrise, Jesus stood on the shore, but the disciples did not recognize Him. "Friends," Jesus called out, "you don't have any fish, do you?" "No," they replied. Jesus told the men to throw their net on the right side of the boat to find fish. As soon as they did, the net was full of fish!

One of the disciples said, "It is the Lord!" When Peter heard that it was the Lord, he jumped into the water and swam ashore. Jesus and the disciples ate breakfast together on the shore.

After breakfast, Jesus asked Peter, "Do you love me?" Peter answered, "Yes, Lord. You know I do!" "Feed my lambs," Jesus told him. A second time Jesus asked Peter, "Do you love me?" "Yes, Lord," Peter responded. "You know that I love you. "Shepherd my sheep," Jesus told him. A third time, Jesus asked, "Peter, do you love me?" Peter was sad that he asked him the third time. Peter responded, "Lord, you know everything; you know that I love you." "Feed my sheep," Jesus said again. After saying this, Jesus told Peter, "Follow me."

Later, Peter was with the other disciples in Jerusalem when the Holy Spirit came and they spoke in many languages. When other people wondered what was happening, Peter stood up and preached to the crowd. He told the people that Jesus was the promised Messiah. Peter told the people to repent of their sin and be baptized. That day about 3,000 people believed in Jesus!

— based on Luke 22:31-34; 54-62; John 21:1-19; Acts 2

MAKE THE CONNECTION

- Peter was a follower of Jesus. He loved Jesus, but when he was tempted, Peter sinned and denied Jesus three times. After His resurrection, Jesus appeared to Peter. Jesus reminded Peter who he was, a follower of Jesus who loved Him. Remind kids that Christians continue to sin because we have a sin nature—we still have hearts that want to sin. One day when Jesus returns, He will make us sinless like Him.

- Emphasize that everyone is responsible for the choices they make, but when a person confesses sin to Jesus and asks for forgiveness, He forgives them. Jesus welcomed Peter, forgave him, and reminded him of his identity and purpose. God called Peter and set him apart for His glory to bring many people to trust in Jesus as Savior. Peter grew in his faith and his knowledge of Jesus, just as all believers do when they live for Jesus.

DEEPER STUDY

- Direct kids to locate Ephesians 4 in their Bibles. Explain that Paul reminded the church in Ephesus what it meant to live out their faith. Invite a volunteer to read Ephesians 4:22-24. Comment that Paul talked about a person taking off his old self and putting on a new one. Paul described living out identity in Jesus like taking off your old identity—broken in sin, and putting on a new identity—child of God!

- Explain that apart from Jesus, we are sinners and we cannot obey God. We are separated from Him, and there is nothing we can do on our own to change that. Thankfully, God sent Jesus to die on the cross for our sin and rise again to defeat death. When we believe in Jesus, He sends the Holy Spirit to live in us and transform everything about us.

- Remind kids that God promises to change us when we believe in Jesus. There are two changes that happen when we trust in Him. The first change is called justification, and it is the change in our status before God. We go from "guilty" because of sin to "not guilty" because of Jesus' perfect righteousness. God changes our identity from broken by sin to child of God.

- The second change takes time, but it is a result of God's power too. This change is called sanctification. It is the change that happens in us little by little to make us think and behave more like Jesus. As we grow we are in the process of becoming what God has already declared us to be. Without the gospel, these amazing changes would be impossible. With God's power through the gospel, anything is possible!

- Instruct the kids to look in verses 25-32 and call out ways believers should act because the Holy Spirit lives inside them. Remark that God's love for us is what causes our obedience. The gospel transforms us. Our minds and hearts change to understand God better and love Him more, and then our behavior changes because of our new thoughts and new desires.

MEMORIZE

- Call attention to the "Key Passage Poster." Point out that kids have worked to memorize all the verses of the passage except verse 2 and verse 3. Explain that the two verses go together. We have waited to learn them now to remind us of our identity before Christ. Knowing who we are in Christ and remembering who we were before Christ reminds us to worship God for saving us and motivates us to tell others about Him.

- Lead the kids to read Ephesians 2:1-3. Call attention to the two verses being much like the verses they just studied in Ephesians 4. These verses tell about a person's life before a new identity in Christ. Then read Ephesians 2:4-7 to show how a person changes when he trusts Jesus.

- Form two groups and lead the groups to face each other. Explain that one group will read the "Key Passage Poster" from the beginning of verse 1 to the first comma or period. The other group will read from that point to the next comma or period. Groups will alternate reading between the punctuation marks all the way to the end of verse 3. Practice the verses this way two or three times. Alternate which group begins the reading.

PRAY

- Post each "Prayer Poster" in a different part of the room. Invite a volunteer to write *Thanks* on one of the sheets. Other volunteers may print *Praise, Help for Others, Help for Ourselves* on other papers.

- Explain that kids will move to different posters and pray quietly to God about the title on the paper. After praying, the child will add her initials to the poster and move to another poster. Encourage the kids to pray thoughtfully, respectfully, and quietly. Close the group in prayer.

INVESTIGATE

You Will Need:
Activity Books, pencils

- Transition kids into small groups, guiding kids to form an older group and a younger group. If you have a large group of either older or younger kids, form groups of about 5 or 6 kids. Distribute the Activity Books and pencils.

- Review last week's daily pages with the group, allowing kids to share what God has been teaching them.

- Complete the Activity Book activities for this session. As kids work, talk with them about today's Bible story and about living out their identity as followers of Jesus.

- Remind kids that following Jesus is not always easy, but it is always worth it. The Holy Spirit helps Christians by guiding us as we live for God's glory.

- Point out the pages for kids to complete at home. Explain that working on the pages can help them learn more about living out their identity. Encourage kids to continue their study during the coming week.

GREEK LETTER POSTERS

You Will Need:
Item 21: "Greek Letters"
Scrap paper, pencils, cardstock, scissors, markers
Optional: glitter, stickers

Teaching Tip:
Some letters do not have close equivalents in the Greek language. Kids whose names begin with those letters can opt to use another initial, a close looking letter, or if needed, just pick a letter they like. The point is learning the ways to grow in their faith and knowledge of Jesus.

- Review the various actions in Ephesians 4:25-32 that Paul encouraged believers to do as they grow in their faith and knowledge of Jesus.

- Explain the New Testament was written mostly in Greek. Show the "Greek Letters." Remark that the Greek alphabet has 24 letters instead of 26 and 7 vowels instead of 5.

- Let each child find the letters that correspond with his first and last initial on the chart. Encourage kids to practice writing their initials in Greek letters on scrap paper. Then suggest they try making their letters large enough to cut out. When kids are satisfied with their letters, they can trace them onto cardstock and cut them out.

- Instruct kids to write on their Greek letters ways believers should act according to the Bible verses they studied during this session. Encourage kids to use different colored markers and different styles of letters as they write.

- Challenge kids to display their Greek letters in their rooms at home to remind them of the ways believers in Jesus can show their changed identity.

STINKY FEET

You Will Need:
Item 22: "Stinky Feet Game Pieces"
Item 23: "Stinky Feet Review Questions"
Sticky notes of any size, tape, a marker, and a bag

To Do:
Tape each "Stinky Feet Game Piece" to the front (non-sticky side) of a different sticky note. On the sticky side of the sticky notes, print a point value: 3, 4, 5, 10, 15, 15, -1, -2, -3, -4. Arrange the game pieces randomly on the wall with the sticky sides toward the wall. Place the "Stinky Feet Review Questions" in the bag.

Teaching Tip:
Using both positive numbers and negative numbers for points means a team can come from behind to win, but if you teach younger children you may want to only use positive numbers and let kids either compete in teams or work together to see how many points they can earn.

- Briefly review today's Bible story with the kids. Remind the group that Peter was a follower of Jesus. He loved Jesus, but when he was tempted, Peter sinned and denied Jesus three times. After His resurrection, Jesus appeared to Peter. Jesus reminded Peter who he was, a follower of Jesus who loved Him. Jesus welcomed Peter, forgave him, and reminded him of his identity and purpose. God called Peter to tell many people about Jesus and taught them to trust in Jesus as Savior. Peter grew in his faith and his knowledge of Jesus, just as all believers do when they live for Jesus.

- Suggest they continue their review by playing "Stinky Feet." Form teams. Explain that the first player on a team will choose a question from the bag. Note for kids that after the question is read, they will have 10 seconds to think about the answer. Once their team has an answer, they may stand up. Once time is called, you will call on the first team member that stood to answer. Once answered correctly, the team member may choose a sticky foot from the wall to reveal the number of points for the team.

- For the next round, a player from the second team chooses the question and play continues. Continue with other review questions. Announce team totals and play again!

INCREASE

You Will Need:
Item 2: "Family Guide"
Item 4: "Key Passage Poster"
Item 24: "Three-Corner Game"

- Lead kids to play a three-corner game. Designate one corner of the room as True, another as False, and another as Not in the Bible story. All players stand in the middle of the playing area.

- Explain that you will read a statement. When you read the statement, say, "You are responsible for your own choices" and let kids move to the corner that tells whether the statement is true, false, or not in today's Bible story. After kids make their choices and move, ask them why they made the choices they did. All kids return to the middle before you read another statement. Keep playing until all the statements have been used.

- Mention that Peter sometimes made good choices and sometimes made wrong choices, but either way, he was the one responsible for them. The good news is that Peter recognized his sin and Jesus forgave Him. Jesus helped Peter grow in his faith and knowledge of Jesus even though he had sinned. Jesus sent the Holy Spirit to help Christians recognize our sin, and guide us as we live for God's glory.

- Call for a volunteer or other leader to lead in prayer thanking God for what He does in the lives of people who trust and follow Him.

- Remind kids of the daily Bible study pages in their activity books. Urge them to use those pages at home.

- Encourage kids to complete this session's "Family Guide" with an adult at home. Distribute a "Family Guide" for this week's session if needed.

- Lead the group to repeat/read Ephesians 2:1-10 from the "Key Passage Poster." Tell kids they will continue working to memorize the key passage during the next session.

Walking in the Spirit

KEY VERSE: "IN WHICH YOU PREVIOUSLY LIVED ACCORDING TO THE WAYS OF THIS WORLD, ACCORDING TO THE RULER OF THE POWER OF THE AIR, THE SPIRIT NOW WORKING IN THE DISOBEDIENT. WE TOO ALL PREVIOUSLY LIVED AMONG THEM IN OUR FLESHLY DESIRES, CARRYING OUT THE INCLINATIONS OF OUR FLESH AND THOUGHTS, AND WE WERE BY NATURE CHILDREN UNDER WRATH AS THE OTHERS WERE ALSO."
EPHESIANS 2:2–3

THROUGH THIS STUDY, KIDS CAN ...

KNOW

The Holy Spirit guides us as we live for God's glory.

UNDERSTAND

The Holy Spirit shows us our sin and helps us make God-honoring choices.

DISCOVER

The Holy Spirit changes the way we think and act to be more like Jesus.

INITIATE

You Will Need:
Item 25: "You've Got Mail"
Tape, newsprint, or other paper for making paper balls, and a large container such as a trash can

To Do:
Cut out, fold, and tape two copies of "You've Got Mail" envelopes.

Teaching Tip:
To make this game more challenging for older kids, mark off three masking tape lines and label them 1, 2, and 3 to indicate how many pieces of mail the team earns if their shot makes it into the trash can. Be sure to make the tape lines are an appropriate distance from the trash can.

YOU'VE GOT MAIL

- Form two teams. Explain that team players will crumple up sheets of paper and try to toss them into the container. Players from both teams may toss at the same time, but only one player from each team can play at a time.

- Note that if a player gets the ball in the container, he earns one piece of mail ("You've Got Mail!") for his team. When a team has collected 10 pieces of mail, the players on the team open the envelopes and arrange the letters to form two words. The team who finishes first is the winner.

- After the game is played explain that most people like to receive mail either on paper, as an email, or as a text message. Mention that in Bible times, people received letters written on scrolls, and the scrolls were often passed around to many groups of people.

- Encourage the kids to listen and find out how mail and the Holy Spirit are important in today's Bible story.

INQUIRE

You Will Need:
Item 4: "Key Passage Poster"
Item 26: "Letter to the Galatians"
Item 27: "Letter to the Ephesians"
Item 28: "Ephesians 2:2 Phrases"
Item 29: "Ephesians 2:3 Phrases"
Bibles, marbles, empty paper towel tubes (cut in half), music, music player, and sticky notes

To Do:
Print the above items and prepare as directed. Bookmark John 16 and Galatians 5 in a Bible.

Teaching Tip:
Use this memory game to help your group remember the fruit of the Spirit. The first three listed are one-syllable words (peace, love, joy). The second set of three are two-syllable words (patience, kindness, goodness). The last set of three are three-syllable words (faithfulness, gentleness, and self-control).

OPEN UP: PASS THE MARBLE

- Direct kids to locate the Table of Contents in their Bibles and find Romans in the list of books. Ask kids to start at Romans, then count 13 books down. Call on a volunteer to tell what the thirteenth book is. *(Philemon)* Explain that Paul wrote each of these 13 Bible books, but they weren't called books when they were first written. These were letters written by Paul to other Christians.

- Give each child a clean paper towel tube. Lead kids to form a circle. Place a marble inside the first player's tube and challenge her to roll the marble carefully to the player on her right while saying the first of the 13 books in the Bible written by Paul (Romans). The next player should transfer the marble to the next player's tube while saying the next book (1 Corinthians). The goal is to transfer the marble thirteen times without dropping it. If a player drops a marble, the next player should begin with Romans again.

- Explain that Paul traveled to many countries and started churches. He also spent time in prison for preaching about Jesus, so Paul used letters to instruct and encourage new believers in new churches. He wanted churches to share their letters with each other to learn more about following Jesus.

• Open the "Letter to the Galatians" and explain that Galatians is the letter Paul wrote to the believers in Galatia. Read the story from the scroll.

TELL THE BIBLE STORY: WALKING IN THE SPIRIT

Paul wrote a letter to the Christians in Galatia. Galatia was a province in Rome, and many of the Christians there were Gentiles, or non-Jews. Paul explained that God changes people who trust in Jesus. God gives them the Holy Spirit, who guides them and gives them power to become more like Jesus. Paul wrote that the Holy Spirit changes the way we think and act. He wanted believers to know that if you let the Holy Spirit guide you, you will do what God wants instead of what you want.

When sin is in control, we do wrong things. We show hatred, jealousy, anger, selfishness, and greed. We fight and get into trouble. People who live like this will not enter God's kingdom. But Jesus frees us from the power of sin. His Holy Spirit lives in us and gives us power to do what is right.

When the Holy Spirit is in control, people choose love, joy, peace, patience, kindness, goodness, faithfulness, gentleness, and self-control. These actions are the fruit of the Spirit—proof that the Spirit is in someone—like how a healthy tree produces fruit. This fruit pleases God. Paul wrote that when we trust in Jesus, we no longer want to do whatever pleases ourselves. The Holy Spirit gives us power to say no to things like hatred, jealousy, anger, selfishness, and greed. The more we know Jesus, the more we will choose actions like joy, kindness, and self-control. We will want to live to please God. Since the Holy Spirit lives in us, we must let the Holy Spirit guide us.

— based on Galatians 5

MAKE THE CONNECTION

• Paul talked about love, joy, peace, patience, kindness, goodness, faithfulness, gentleness, and self-control as the fruit of the Spirit. When we believe in Jesus, the Holy Spirit naturally begins to grow those attributes in our lives. Jesus taught that you can tell who is a true follower of Him based on what their lives look like. (See Matt. 7:15-20.)

• The Holy Spirit changes the way we think and act to be more like Jesus. Just like an apple seed takes a long time to grow into an apple tree and produces apples, it takes time for us to grow in our faith. But when the "seed" of the gospel is growing in your life, the "fruit" your life produces will be the fruit of the Spirit: love, joy, peace, patience, kindness, goodness, faithfulness, gentleness, and self-control.

- When we trust in Jesus, the Holy Spirit begins to change us. Paul told the believers at the church in Galatia how to recognize that God is working in someone's life. People who are saved by Jesus become more like Him, and the Holy Spirit gives them power to say no to sin and to live in a way that pleases God.

DEEPER STUDY

- Explain that Paul wrote many important letters to the churches that kids can find and read about in their Bibles. Open the second scroll ("Letter to the Ephesians") as you explain that Paul also wrote a letter to the believers in Ephesus and you have part of it on your scroll. Read it aloud.

  From Paul to the church in Ephesus:

  Imitate God as dearly loved children, and walk in love. Jesus loved us and gave himself for us. Sin should not be heard about among you. Foolish words and crude joking are not suitable, but rather give thanks. Control your life with love just as Jesus loved us and gave Himself for us.

  Don't let anyone deceive you with empty arguments. God's judgment is coming on the disobedient because of these things. Don't partner with them. You were once in darkness, but now you are light in the Lord. Live as children of light—for the fruit of the light consists of all goodness, righteousness and truth. Don't participate in the fruitless works of darkness and sin.

  Pay careful attention to how you live—not as unwise people but as wise—making use of every opportunity to do good. Don't be foolish, but understand what the Lord's will is. Be filled with the Spirit: speaking to one another in psalms, hymns, and songs to the Lord, making music with your heart to the Lord. Always give thanks for everything to God in the name of Jesus. Do these things because of your love for Jesus Christ.

  –based on Ephesians 5:1-21

- Ask if kids heard any similar words in these two letters? (Holy Spirit, fruit, and so forth) Mention that the Bible helps us know at least three things about the Holy Spirit: The Holy Spirit comforts us, shows us our sin, and guides us as we live for God's glory.

- Ask a volunteer to read John 16:13. Explain that Jesus told His followers that the Spirit would guide them. Ask another child to read John 16:8 aloud. Comment that this verse tells us that the Holy Spirit shows people their sin.

- Explain that Galatians 5:16-17 tells us that the Spirit helps believers make God-honoring choices. Then in Galatians 5:22-25 we find that the Holy Spirit changes the way we think and act so that we will be more like Jesus.

- Guide boys and girls to locate Ephesians 5:15 in their Bibles. Ask them what the verse instructs them to do. *(Live wisely.)* Inquire how they could do this, reminding them that the Holy Spirit guides believers to make God-honoring choices.

- Ask how Ephesians 5:19 suggests believers should act. Reassure kids that they can still sing and hear other music, but they also need to spend time encouraging each other in Christ. Let kids share what action is encouraged in verse 20.

MEMORIZE

- Call attention to the "Key Passage Poster." Lead the group to read aloud the entire passage together. Remind kids that they began learning verses 2-3 during the last session, but the group will continue memorizing them this week. Point out that verse 1 is important to remember as they begin verse 2, because it is really the first part of the sentence continued in verse 2. Mention that verses 1-3 all tell what being dead in sin is like.

- Point out the Bible-verse phrases around the room. Explain that you will play music as kids walk around the room. Note that when the music stops, kids will place a hand on the poster nearest them. More than one person may touch the same poster.

- Play the music for a few seconds. Stop the music and wait as kids move to different posters. Call attention to the numbers on the posters. Explain that kids at each poster will read the posters in number order to practice Ephesians 2:2. (If no one is at a poster, invite the whole group to read it.) Let kids touching the first poster read first, then the second, and so forth. Repeat the activity for several rounds.

- Cover the numbers on the poster with sticky notes. Play the game again and let students try to remember the verse order without them. Change the posters to the "Ephesians 2:3" set and play again.

PRAY

- Suggest kids follow the example in Ephesians 5:20 by thanking God in prayer. Explain that you will mention different prompts, then wait as kids pray silent prayers of thanks. Remind kids to sit respectfully and quietly as they pray silently. For younger kids, use comments such as: Thank God for something you like outdoors. Thank God for the way He takes care of you. Thank God for one of your favorite people. Thank God for your favorite Bible story. Thank God for the Bible. End with "Amen."

INVESTIGATE

You Will Need:
Activity Books, pencils

- Transition kids into small groups, forming an older group and a younger group. If you have a large group of either older or younger kids, form groups of about 5 or 6 kids. Distribute the Activity Books and pencils.

- Complete the activity book pages for this session. As kids work, talk with them about today's Bible story and discuss the fruit of the Spirit.

- Point out the pages for kids to complete at home this week. Explain that working on the pages can help them learn more about walking in the Spirit and living for Jesus. Encourage kids to continue their study during the coming week.

SECRET MESSAGE WRIST CUFFS

You Will Need:
Cardboard tubes cut into 2-inch lengths, scissors, pens or fine markers, 3 ½ inch lengths of ⅛ inch elastic, glue or tape, and various patterned papers cut into two-inch widths

To Do:
Cut the two-inch widths of paper into approximate lengths to wrap around the tubes.

- Review what kids learned from Paul's letters about the Holy Spirit and how the Spirit helps believers.

- Suggest kids make wrist cuffs with secret messages about the Holy Spirit inside them. Point out that no one can see the messages while the cuffs are being worn unless the wearer shares the messages.

- Give each kid a section of a cardboard tube. Guide the kids to make one cut so that the roll spreads slightly apart. Encourage the kids to write their messages inside the roll. They might write things such as, "The Holy Spirit comforts us, shows us our sin, and guides us as we live for God's glory" or "With the Holy Spirit's help, Christians can say no to sin and follow Jesus." Kids might also choose to list the fruit of the Spirit from Galatians 5:22-23.

- After kids finish their messages, assist them in stapling the ends of a length of elastic to each side of the cuff opening. Be sure the staple ends face outward. Let kids tape or glue patterned paper to the outside of the cuff, being sure to cover the ends of the elastic. Trim paper away from the edge as needed.

- Point out to kids that the message is secret, but they can share the message either by telling others or letting people read it.

HOW DO YOU STACK UP?

You Will Need:
Paper, pencils, stopwatch or watch with a second hand, plastic cups
Optional: yardstick

To Do:
Read Ephesians 2:2-3 before the session and decide what phrases you will use in the game and what key words you can leave out for kids to answer.

Teaching Tip:
Consider posting the "Ephesians 2:2" and "Ephesians 2:3" posters used earlier in the session. After a few rounds of play, remove the posters.

- Lead kids to repeat together as much of Ephesians 2:2-3 from memory as they can. Challenge kids to play a game to help them continue memorizing the verses.

- Form pairs of kids. (If you have an uneven number, three kids can work on a team.) Give each kid a piece of paper and a pencil. Explain that you will read a phrase from the verses, leaving out an important word from the phrase. Tell kids they will each write down what they think is the missing word. Partners may talk together. When you call time, kids reveal their answers. Every pair that answered correctly is awarded one cup.

- Do a practice round to be sure kids understand the directions. Direct the kids to set aside the cups they earn. Continue to read a phrase from the verses, leaving out one or two words. Allow a few seconds for kids to think and write their answers. Again, award pairs a cup for every right answer. Keep going until you only have two or three minutes left to play.

- Announce that kids will now work with their partners to build the highest tower they can with the number of cups they earned. Explain that each pair can build the tower any way they want. Point out that using a good design might mean that a pair with fewer cups could still win the game.

- Time the kids for about 2 minutes. When you call time, every pair must stop work immediately.

- Check all the towers. Measure them with a yardstick if needed. Declare the winner, but praise everyone for the work they have done.

- Lead the group to repeat Ephesians 2:3-4 together by memory.

INCREASE

You Will Need:
Item 2: "Family Guide"
Item 4: "Key Passage Poster"

To Do:
Cover the "Key Passage Poster" with a sheet of paper or a bed sheet.
Be ready to lead the song "God Is So Good" without accompaniment or locate music to use.

- Review today's Bible story by asking kids to name three ways the Holy Spirit helps believers in Jesus. *(Comforts us, shows us our sin, and guides us as we live for God's glory)* Ask what two Bible books they learned about today and what form those books had in Bible times. *(Galatians and Ephesians; letters on scrolls)* Call on volunteers to tell ways people can act and think more like Jesus.

- Remind kids that the Holy Spirit helps Christians grow to look more like Jesus. Ask which of the three ways mentioned might not be as enjoyable the other two. *(The Holy Spirit shows us our sin.)* Invite kids to share ideas about why it is good for the Holy Spirit to show believers their sin. Then ask for ideas of things people might want to start doing when they follow Jesus. Continue by asking ideas of ways the Holy Spirit guides people. *(Prayer, reading the Bible, choosing to say kind words to others, and so forth)*

- Read Ephesians 5:20 aloud. If your group is familiar with the song "God Is So Good," lead kids to sing the song as their prayer of thanks to God. If they do not know the song, let them take turns telling things they are thankful to God for.

- Remind kids to complete this week's activity pages in the Younger or Older Kids Activity Book. Emphasize the daily Bible study portions, explaining that kids can read a Bible passage, do a short activity, and pray as they follow the directions. Point out that doing so is one way the Holy Spirit can work in a person's life.

- Encourage kids to complete this session's "Family Guide" in their Activity Book with an adult at home. Distribute a "Family Guide" for this week's session if needed.

- Show the covered "Key Passage Poster." Lead kids to repeat the first verse (Eph. 2:1) together by memory. Remove the cover from the first verse only and let kids check if they were right. Do the same with verse 2 and again with verse 3. Then uncover the entire poster. Urge kids to try repeating the verse by memory, but allow them to look at the poster as needed. Tell the group they will work on saying the entire passage by memory during the next session. Play "You've Got Mail" again as kids are waiting to be picked up.

Living on Mission

KEY VERSE: "WE ARE HIS WORKMANSHIP, CREATED IN CHRIST JESUS FOR GOOD WORKS, WHICH GOD PREPARED AHEAD OF TIME FOR US TO DO." EPHESIANS 2:10

THROUGH THIS STUDY, KIDS CAN ...

KNOW

God has given us everything we need to live on mission with Him.

UNDERSTAND

We have a real enemy who wants to discourage us from fulfilling our mission.

DISCOVER

Our mission is to make disciples of all nations by the power of the Holy Spirit.

INITIATE

You Will Need:
Item 30: "Walking, Walking"

To Do:
Post the sign in the room.

Teaching Tip:
If you teach a small group, go around the circle more than once. Kids choose a different way to walk each time they take a turn, but they must recall the order of all the walking steps.

WALK ON

- Welcome kids as they arrive.

- Lead kids to stand in a circle. Explain that kids will walk in place as they play a game. Begin the game by saying, "I'm going on a walk. I'm going to walk by..." naming a way to walk (refer to the sign if needed). Begin walking in place in that manner and lead the group do the same. After a few seconds, lead the child next to you to repeat the sentence, "I'm going on a walk, and I'm going to walk by..." and name his choice. All kids walk three or four steps the way he chose, followed by another three or four steps the way you chose. The third kid names a different way to walk. Kids walk in place their way, the second way, and your way. Continue, adding a way to walk with each kid and repeat all the ways, in order, that were done before.

- Explain that in today's session, kids will learn about living on mission with God. Note for them that living on mission is not about physical footsteps but about telling and teaching others about Jesus no matter where they go.

LIVING ON MISSION

INQUIRE

You Will Need:
Item 4: "Key Passage Poster"
Item 31: "A Soldier and His Armor"

To Do:
Mark Matthew 28, Acts 1, and Ephesians 6 in a Bible.

Teaching Tip:
Kids who have not attended all sessions may be unsure of the memory passage. Consider asking an entire line to repeat the verse together and then asking the other line to repeat it. Then let one line slide to the right and continue as directed but with the whole lines repeating the verse.

OPEN UP: PASS IT ON

- Invite kids to stand shoulder to shoulder. You will whisper an exciting message to the first kid, who will whisper it to the next person in line. The message will travel down the line until it gets to the last person. The last person will share what he heard.

- Comment that kids were given an important message to share with the person next to them. They had to be careful to share the right message. Ask how they think the group did. Explain that in today's Bible story Jesus gave His disciples an important job. He wanted them to tell everyone to trust Jesus as their Lord and Savior. That is a great message to share!

- Open your Bible to Matthew 28. Tell the following Bible story in your own words.

TELL THE BIBLE STORY: JESUS GAVE THE GREAT COMMISSION

After Jesus had been raised from the dead, He met with His disciples over the next 40 days. During that time, Jesus told them even more about God's kingdom. Then Jesus' eleven disciples went to a mountain in Galilee.

When the disciples saw Jesus, some of them worshiped Him. But some of the disciples still doubted. Then Jesus went up to them and said, "All authority has been given to Me in heaven and on earth." Jesus is God the Son; He always had authority. But after Jesus died on the cross and rose from the dead, God gave Him all authority in heaven and on earth. Jesus is the King over all creation, and He rules over God's kingdom.

Jesus gave the disciples—and everyone who follows Him—a job to do. He said, "Go into all the world and preach the gospel. Make disciples of people from every nation." A disciple is a follower. Jesus wants His followers to tell people all over the world how to be rescued from sin and death by trusting in Jesus' death and resurrection. Then those people who believe would become disciples of Jesus too.

Jesus also said, "Baptize them in the name of the Father and of the Son and of the Holy Spirit." When believers are baptized, they show the world that they have turned from sin and trusted in Jesus as their Savior. Jesus continued, "Teach them to obey everything I have commanded you." Disciples who love Jesus will want to obey Him. Then Jesus said, "Remember this: I am always with you, until the very end of the age."

Some time later, Jesus also said to His disciples, "You will receive power when the Holy Spirit has come on you. You will be My witnesses in Jerusalem, in all Judea and Samaria, and to the ends of the earth."

After Jesus said these things, He went up into heaven. The disciples watched Jesus until a cloud hid Him from their sight. All of the sudden, two men appeared. The men were wearing white clothes. These men asked the disciples, "Men of Galilee, why do you stand looking up into heaven? This Jesus, who has been taken from you into heaven, will come again. He will return in the same way that you have seen Him going into heaven."

— based on Matthew 28:16-20 and Acts 1:4-14

LIVING ON MISSION

MAKE THE CONNECTION

- Jesus died on the cross to rescue us from sin and rose again to defeat death. That news is too good not to share. Jesus wants His followers to teach people everywhere about Jesus so they will trust in Him as their Lord and Savior.

- Jesus gave the disciples the Great Commission, but it wasn't just for them. It is a command for all of us. Every person who believes in Jesus has a responsibility to share the gospel—the good news about Jesus. Our mission is to make disciples of all nations by the power of the Holy Spirit.

DEEPER STUDY

- Explain that God has given us everything we need to live on mission with Him. Direct kids to Ephesians 6:10-20. Read these verses aloud and discuss them. Comment that these verses teach us about the armor of God. The armor of God is not a physical armor that we carry around or wear. The armor Paul talked about was his way of communicating the protection God gives believers to live on mission.

- Display the "Soldier and His Armor" image. Lead a volunteer to read Ephesians 6:14 aloud. Ask kids to identify the first piece of armor (belt of truth). Print the title on the line pointing to the belt. Explain that the belt was the first piece of armor a soldier put on because it strengthened his core to help him carry his armor and still fight. Christians can put on the belt of truth by believing that whatever God says is what is true.

- Ask what the second piece of armor in the same verse is. (chest armor or breastplate) Print the name on the blank. Mention that the chest armor protected the body's main organs. This piece of armor represents changing one's actions into what God wants them to be.

- Guide kids to find the next piece of armor in Ephesians 6:15. Print the name on the blank. Tell kids that soldiers' sandals were made of leather and had bumps on the bottom to help the soldiers stand firm. Having on shoes makes one ready for action. For Christians, the shoes show they are ready to go tell about Jesus.

- Lead kids to find the next piece of armor in verse 16. Print the name on the blank. Explain that a soldier's shield was large enough to cover his whole body and was made of wood covered with fabric and leather with iron edges. They protected the body from swords and flaming arrows. The shield of faith means having trust and faith in God no matter what.

- Continue with verse 17 for the next piece of armor. Explain that a Roman soldier's helmet was made of iron to protect the brain. The helmet of salvation helps protect the mind of a believer and what is good and right to think about.

- The last piece of armor is also listed in verse 17. Ask what it is. (sword of the Spirit) The sword that Paul wrote about was small and very sharp with double cutting edges. Paul described this sword as the Word of God. Comment that the Bible is how we fight back against temptation.

- Remark in addition to the armor, we can always rely on prayer. Read Ephesians 6:18 aloud. Comment that we have a real enemy who wants to discourage us from fulfilling our mission. Our enemy is not physical, or made of flesh and blood. Our enemy is Satan. He cannot take away our salvation, but he wants us to fail at obeying God and to keep us from telling other people about Jesus. Thankfully, God gives us what we need to stand strong against evil and continue living on mission with Him.

MEMORIZE

- Repeat Ephesians 2:10 as a group. Remind kids they memorized this verse at the beginning of this study. Lead the group to say the entire 10 verses of Ephesians 2:1-10 together.

- Lead kids to form two equal lines with each kid facing someone from the opposing line.

- Challenge the group in one of the lines to repeat the verse to the person directly in front of him. Kids may look at the "Key Passage Poster" as needed. Then invite kids from the second line to repeat the verse back to the kids across from them.

- Direct one line to slide right one step so kids are facing new partners. Since one person in each line will not have a partner now, tell one kid without a partner to move to the other end of the line. Together repeat verse 2. Encourage kids in one line to say the verse to their partners and then let the partners say the verse. Guide the kids in the other line to slide to new partners. Ask one child without a partner to move to the other end of the line. Continue this way until kids have repeated each verse of the passage.

- End with the entire group repeating Ephesians 2:1-10 together.

PRAY

- Remind kids that Paul told believers to be ready to fight a spiritual battle each and every day. We can fight the battle against evil each day through prayer.

- Lead the group in prayer, thanking God for His goodness, faithfulness and love. Ask Him to help your group put on the full armor of God each day. Pray that God would guide us through the Holy Spirit to fight the enemy and continue living on mission—expanding God's kingdom and making disciples.

LIVING ON MISSION

INVESTIGATE

You Will Need:
Activity Books, pencils

- Transition kids into small groups, forming an older group and a younger group. If you have a large group of either older or younger kids, form groups of about 5 or 6 kids. Distribute the Activity Books and pencils.

- Complete the activity book activities for this session. Remind kids that our identity as followers of Jesus is to live on mission with Him. Our mission is to make disciples of all nations by the power of the Holy Spirit.

- Point out the pages for kids to complete at home. Encourage kids to continue their study during the coming week.

MARBLE MAZES

You Will Need:
Item 4: "Key Passage Poster"
Paper plates, drinking straws, scissors, tape, and marbles or round wooden beads

Teaching Tip:
Flexible bend straws make good corners for the mazes but straight straws work too.

Emphasize the memory aspect of the game as kids play. Praise them for the work they have done memorizing the passage as you encourage them to practice saying the whole thing. Some kids may need to adjust their mazes after a trial run.

- Suggest kids create marble mazes to help them practice the key passage.

- Present the paper plates, straws, and tape. Explain that kids can design their own mazes using the straws to form the paths. Mention that kids may have specific start and stop points, or they may want to make the maze where it can be done in a loop. Show the width of the marble or bead so kids can be sure to make their paths wide enough for them. Point out that having several turns in the maze can make it more fun to navigate.

- When the mazes are complete, kids try to keep their marbles moving in the mazes as they repeat the Key Passage. Point out that if they need to read the "Key Passage Poster," they will have to take their eyes off the maze and may drop the marbles. Challenge the kids to repeat as much of the passage as they can before they either drop the marble from the maze or forget the next part of the passage. Urge the kids to play the game over and over, reinforcing what they have learned.

DRESS THE SOLDIER

You Will Need:
Item 32: "Dress the Soldier Questions"
Poster board, 2 each of these items: belts, large shirts, large shoes, caps, and Bibles

To Do:
Cut two shield shapes from the poster board.

Teaching Tip:
If your group is small, let each team dress a chair using the items.

- Remind the kids that our mission is to make disciples of all nations by the power of the Holy Spirit. God has given us everything we need to live on mission for Him. In Ephesians 6:10-20 Paul lists as a soldier's armor the spiritual gifts the Holy Spirit provides to Christians. Guide kids to scan Ephesians 6:10-20 and review the six pieces of armor listed and what each one represents.

- Invite the kids to play a game to help them remember these pieces of spiritual armor and what they mean. (belts: belt of truth; shirts: breastplate of righteousness; shoes: shoes of peace; poster board shield: shield of faith; cap: helmet of salvation; Bible: the sword of the Spirit)

- Form two teams. Choose one kid from each team to be the soldier. The two soldiers stand beside you facing their teams. Explain that you will alternate teams as you ask questions from today's study. When a team answers correctly, a team member can choose one item and put it on the soldier. Play moves to the other team. If a team member answers the question incorrectly, the question moves to the other team. The first team to have their soldier wearing at least five items is the winner.

- If time allows, change teams and play again.

- Remind kids that we have a real enemy who wants to discourage us from fulfilling our mission.

- The Holy Spirit helps Christians to resist Satan and guides us to live on mission for God's glory. Emphasize that Christians can live on mission knowing they have the armor of God to help them resist Satan, because God is more powerful than Satan ever will be.

INCREASE

You Will Need:
Item 2: "Family Guide"
A ball, music and music player

- Remind the kids that Jesus gave the disciples the Great Commission. This is the mission for every person who believes in Jesus—to make disciples of all nations by the power of the Holy Spirit.

- Instruct the kids to form a circle with each kid standing behind the kid in front of him. Play music.

- As music plays, pass the ball around the circle by passing it over the head of one player, between the legs of the next one, over the head, between the legs, and so forth. Stop the music and prompt the kid holding the ball to share one way she can tell someone about Jesus. Continue as time allows.

- After a few rounds, change the assignment to telling a country where people need to know about Jesus. Later in the game, change the assignment to telling a piece of God's armor for Christians.

- Remind the kids that the Activity Books have pages to be completed during the coming week. Encourage the kids to not only complete their pages for the week, but to go back through the book and review the pages they have completed and what God has taught them.

- Encourage kids to complete this session's "Family Guide" in their Activity Book with an adult at home. Distribute a "Family Guide" for this week's session if needed.

- Play the ball pass game again. This time as kids pass the ball, they will say Ephesians 2:1-10 all together. Challenge the kids to say the passage without stopping. If the ball is dropped, kids can keep saying the passage while one kid retrieves the ball. Praise kids for what they have learned.